7 Ingredients To An Effective Prayer Life

ACKNOWLEDGEMENTS

First and foremost, I would like to thank God for being my creator and my all in all. To my beautiful daughter whom I love dearly, thanks for the love and support; you give continually. To my parents, my aunt, Pastor Regina Holmes, and my extended family thanks for being there when I needed you the most. To WofGod Inc. Staff and Affiliates, thanks so much for all you do to hold my arms up I could not do what I do without you. To my Daughters of Distinction staff you all rock… Thanks for all you do; now we can breathe a little. Even though the ride is just beginning, don't get to comfortable. To the two awesome vessels of God, who did the forward and review of this book. Prophet Meghan Rivers, Light of Life International Ministries, and Apostle Dr. Rebecca Murray, Portering The Glory International, Inc. Your contribution to this project is so appreciated. Lastly, but not least, thanks to all the co-authors of this book, I am so Godly proud of you. The best is yet to come for each and every one of you. God stretched us and made us better vessels of honor for His sake. If I have forgotten anyone, charge to my head and not my heart. Thank you, thank you, and thank you!

With Love

Trena

FOREWORD

"But speak thou the things which become sound doctrine (Titus 2:1 KJV)*."*

There is a clarion call today for all hearts to be turned to the heart of the Father. We are living in an age where people are desperate for a way out of the issues, addictions, and crisis that have kept them bound far too long.

Seven Ingredients to an Effective Prayer Life is a beacon shining with practical truths on how to be focused in Christ. So, that you can be confident of your direction and alignment with His will.

In this finely crafted work, you will find biblical keys and tools for helping you turn away from misaligned thoughts, words, or deeds. You will be taught how to open your heart with sincere intimacy toward the Father and your spirit will be set ablaze with the desire to maximize your prayer life on the behalf of others.

The word of God tells us that we hold treasure in earthen vessels (2 Corinthians 4:7 KJV). In addition, God also expresses in His word how he has always provided a purpose, plan, and in times of a need an escape to make sure, we keep on toward the prize of beholding Him face to face. *"God, for whom and through whom everything was made, chose to bring many children into glory. And it was only right that he should make Jesus, through his suffering, a perfect leader, fit to bring them into their salvation…Since he himself has gone through suffering and testing, he is able to help us when we are being tested* (Hebrews 2:10-18 NLT)*."*

Seven Ingredients to an Effective Prayer Life is a precious alabaster box filled with the fragrance of God's glory through the lives of Wives, single mothers, grandmothers, business owners, teachers, counselors, accomplished writers and ministers. These teachings and testimonies will encourage you on how to press in and persevere in spending time with God. For it is in God's secret place that our hearts are trained to hear from the Father with confidence and assurance to work out our own salvation.

This collection of practical truths, precepts, and prayers are the fruitful results of how focusing on God and seeking His face and plan transforms your thoughts, words, and deeds so you see yourself as He sees you: *covered with righteousness and grace.*

I believe as you read and meditate on the treasures in **Seven Ingredients to an Effective Prayer Life** you will receive a fresh revelation that you are: Called, appointed, anointed and positioned for purposeful influence and power in the earth. Let the Son arise in your heart today so you may fulfill your destiny and His mandate for the world!

Dr. Rebecca M. Murray
Portering The Glory International, Inc.
Edinburg, Virginia
www.porteringtheglory.org

PREFACE

In the latest publication from Daughters of Distinction, "Seven Ingredients to an Effective Prayer Life (Volumes Three through Five)", the contributors seamlessly take readers on a journey of the continual process of sanctification in God's eyes. The writers provide plenty of scriptural evidence, for the lasting fruit that a prayer life rooted firmly in repentance, righteousness, and holiness yields. Beginning with the practice of repentance as phase one of living a lifestyle pleasing to the Lord; contributors have masterfully illustrated their own unique experiences with what can best be described as a 'pouring out' of all that is and has become unfruitful in each of our lives. By participating in the deliberate act of repentance, each of us, by the estimation of each writer, is now able to have access to the abundant life intended by our Creator. Challenged to perform a "self-inspection," of hearts and minds, readers determine whether the foundational principal of repentance has truly taken root in our respective lives. In volume four, participants are motivated to live a life of righteousness before God and each other. Clearly, each of the authors in this volume, recognize that over time believers can grow "weary in well doing," and the overarching theme in each writing is simply this - "Do not give up!" The writers are able to empathize with the readers by providing at times personal testimonies of the vicissitudes of life. Righteousness may seem like it is impossible to attain, however, the resounding message found in these pages, is that there is an expectation of heaven for the kind of lifestyle only exhibited in and through righteousness. While righteousness leaves no room for deviations, each of these writers substantiates the truth found in the gospel of Matthew - *"seek ye first the kingdom of God and*

his righteousness and all these things will be added unto you."
In the final volume, contributors tackle the subject of holiness.
It is clear that an effective prayer life systematically built on the
consistent application of repentance and righteousness will yield a
lifestyle of perfected holiness. Holiness, while clearly an attribute
of Divinity, is also the expectation of heaven for each of us. As
Christian believers our declaration that there is no God like our
God, should compel each of us to strive to be just like Him. With
personal accounts of lives transformed by a consistent prayer life
and a fervent and active pursuit of the holiness of God, the writers
entice readers to join them in their pursuit to please the Lord. It is
interesting to note, that an effective prayer life with the use of these
three principles serves as acts of worship that not only produce
positive results in our lives, but also is concurrently pleasing to
God. In summation this amalgamation of writings from some of
the Kingdom's finest writers leaves its readers with the following
statement of truth, "To err is human, but to REPENT is both
RIGHTEOUS and HOLY before our God!"

Prophet Meghan N. Rivers, M.Div
Light of Life International Ministries
www.lightoflifeintlministries.com

VOLUME III - REPENTANCE

TABLE OF CONTENTS

VOLUME III REPENTANCE

CHAPTER 1

An About Face

To speak to a thing, one must understand a thing. To understand a thing, one must give proper time and research to it. Solomon states, **"Wisdom is the principal thing; therefore, get wisdom: and with all thy getting get understanding."** (Proverbs 4:7 King James Version KJV) Oftentimes in life, particularly as it pertains to the Word of God, we tend to speak and respond prematurely without giving adequate time, thought, and study to the subject at hand. As a result, we don't reap the full benefits of the information nor do we experience the fullness of what God has for us in return. In order to have a real understanding of true repentance, we must study the topic in relationship to its original context of Scripture so that we can properly apply it to our lives.

Many of us will remember during our childhood years the discipline we received for less than favorable behavior and hearing the words of our parents say to us, "This is going to hurt me more than it hurt you!" For many of us, a discussion immediately ensued explaining the reason for such disciplinary action. At the time, the words of our parents sounded contradictory and their action seemed like anything but love. We did not understand or appreciate what they had done, much less what they said. However, being older, wiser, and now having children of our own their words and actions now make all the sense in the world. We now realize that although the correction was hurtful, it was necessary because our parents cared about our well-being, our future, and our success. They loved us; they wanted the best for us. ***"For the moment all discipline seems painful rather than pleasant, but later it yields the peaceful fruit of righteousness to those who have been trained by it."*** **(Hebrews 12:11 English Standard Version ESV).** Simply put, right discipline yields true righteousness for those who will submit to it. Additionally, we now recognize correction without understanding is just activity; in other words, discipline without understanding is behavior prone to repetition.

Merriam-Webster (n.d.) defines understanding[1] as "a mental grasp; comprehension." Growing up, our parents wanted to ensure we comprehended the "why" in our correction so we would not commit the same offense again, and so it is with the Father. **Proverbs 3:12** tells us that He corrects those He loves. When we get off course, He steers us back on track via the path of correction. However, as with children it is not enough for us to acknowledge our wrongdoing by saying, *"I'm sorry."* The Father is not looking for us to clear our conscious. He wants us to make a conscious choice to change our ways. Our heart and mind must come into proper alignment and make an agreement to change. Otherwise, we are inclined to repeat the same sinful behaviors. True repentance requires a sincere, earnest change.

Often times when we hear the word, repentance, the first thought that tends to come to mind is expressing genuine remorse or contrition for our wrongdoing or sin. Similarly, we default to the same interpretation when reading about repentance in the Word of God. *"For my thoughts are not your thoughts, neither are your ways my ways, saith the Lord."* **(Isaiah 55:8 KJV)**. Since our finite minds cannot comprehend the mind of the infinite God, we cannot afford to default to our limited way of thinking when it comes to His Word. In **Revelations 4:1 (KJV)**, God instructed John to *"Come up hither."* Some may ask where was the place John was to come up to. So, that John could fully understand what was to come thereafter, he had to raise his level of thinking; his consciousness had to come up to God's level. We must do the same thing. We must embrace and approach the Word, which is God **(John 1:1)**, in His fullness. Thus, to understand God's real intent, His plan concerning repentance, we must study it in relationship to its context in Scripture.

The New Testament is filled with examples of a people called to a place of repentance. John the Baptist, preaching in the wilderness of Judea proclaimed to the people, *"...Repent ye: for the kingdom of heaven is at hand."* (**Matthew 3:2 KJV**).

"Now after that John was put in prison, Jesus came into Galilee, preaching the gospel of the kingdom of God, And saying , The time is fulfilled, and the kingdom of God is at hand: repent ye, and believe the gospel." **(Mark 1:14-15 KJV)**. In both instances of Scripture, the definition of the word translated as "repent" is not in keeping with Merriam-Webster's definition. Although repentance does involve feelings of regret and remorse, the Father desires much more from us than emotional expressions. Feelings of guilt and remorse are only the first step.

The King James Version New Testament Greek Lexicon word for repent is *Metanoeo*[2], which means "to change one's mind or to change one's mind for better, heartily to amend with abhorrence of one's past sins." The New Testament references this application of repent thirty-two (32) times in scripture. In other words, when a person repents from sin his/her thought process or way of thinking must turn from where it is to where it needs to be. This is the second step. The mindset must do a complete 180 degree turn, an about face. Our emotions, which often times fail us, can no longer be the sole determining factor in our act of repentance. As we turn from our sinful ways, we must change our mindset because it is not about what we say; it is about how we live and the choices we make in life determine how we live. As in the words of Martin Luther, "*To do so no more is the truest repentance.*" This is essential for true deliverance and healing to take place. It brings us back into right standing with Him. This is true repentance.

A reformed mindset is essential because when we change our mind, our behavior follows suit. Our direction, decisions, and dimension all change. We no longer have the same posture concerning sin. We no longer desire to embrace sin, enjoy sin, entertain sin, or engage in sin. We turn away from sin and turn towards righteousness. We think differently, we feel differently, we hear differently, we see differently, we speak differently, and we choose to do differently. We realize that it is not about the good works (the dead works) that we do, but rather the sinful things that we turn from and repent of that bring us back into right relationship with God. Moreover, we understand that the longer we take turning back to the Father in true repentance, the more difficult it becomes.

Thus, we must be active in our repentance, not passive. We do not want to lose sight of our need to repent. We don't want anything to clog the lifeline between Him and us. We recognize that He is our intravenous (IV) drip and we cannot make it without Him. We want to stay connected to the vine; we want to remain in intimate fellowship with the Father. Thus, the moment we fall short, we want to confess and repent. Otherwise, we become as the church of Laodicea described in the Book of Revelations that became lukewarm and indifferent by God's repeated call to repentance and restoration.

The Laodicean church was comprised of a people whose hope and trust were in material possessions. They relished their material prosperity. In turn, it gave them a false sense of security and freedom. **Revelations 3:15- 16 (KJV)** further describes them as a people who were neither hot nor cold in their love for God, just lukewarm. In other words, they were neither on fire for God or stone cold against God; they were straight down the middle, which is descriptive of many in the body of Christ today, in particular the Westernized church. For their indifference, the Lord had no pleasant words for them. Of the seven (7) churches described in Revelations, this was the only church that did not receive a commendation. Instead, He only offered words of discontentment; He told them He would spew them out of His mouth **(Revelations 3:16 KJV)**. However, inasmuch as their behavior repulsed Him, God extended them the ultimate opportunity for change.

Under the function of the Holy Spirit, John said in **Revelations 3:18** that the Lord "counseled" them to do an about face because although the Laodiceans were physically rich, they were spiritually poor. Therefore, instead of purchasing real gold, He exhorted them to buy the gold that had been through the refiner's fire for gold processed in the refiner's fire is proven³. It would allow them to become a reflection of Him that not only He could see, but others could see also. Instead of acquiring the popular soft, black wool garments manufactured in Laodicea He recommended they buy white raiment signifying righteousness for they had been improperly clothed long enough.⁴ Lastly, instead of purchasing the eye salve they produced and sold He implored them to obtain the spiritual eye salve from Him so they could really see; no longer walking in spiritual blindness, but with spiritual sight.⁵ Everything they prided themselves on as a city, He admonished and corrected. He admonished them because He loved them and He appealed to them to repent with great zeal because He wanted to restore them. This is evidenced through the Word of God, *"To him that overcometh will I grant to sit with me in my throne, even as I also overcame, and am set down with my Father in his throne."* **(Revelations 3:21 KJV).** For those that would choose to conquer their sin and incline their ear to what the Spirit of the Lord was saying, they would sit with Him on His throne. Talk about restoration!

The Lord wanted to restore the Laodicean church back to a right place in Him, and so it is with us. The Lord takes no pleasure or glory in having us live in sin. He offers repentance so that we can be with Him and reap all that He has for us in return. This is why it is vitally important we understand His true intent and plan concerning repentance. The Father wants us with Him; He longs for us to be in Him; He wants us restored back to Him! Thus, He does not want us to be slothful or half-hearted in our act of repentance. He wants us to be passionate and quick in our approach so we can be back in right fellowship with Him, completely unhindered by our known and unknown sin. He desires for us to willingly open the door where He patiently stands saying, ***"Behold, I stand at the door, and knock: if any man hear my voice, and open the door, I will come in to him, and will sup with him, and he with me."*** **(Revelations 3:20 KJV)**. Let us make the choice today to open the door, the door of our heart, for change: a change of heart and a change of mind. Let us do an about face.

PRAYER

Heavenly Father, I thank You for another day that You have blessed us with because it is another opportunity that we can get it right. I thank You for Your grace, Your mercy, and Your unconditional love, a love that Your Word says we can never be separated from. I come to You on behalf of a people, a nation, and a world that has lost sight of our need of You. We have placed everything before You forgetting it is because of You that we are here. Forgive us, Lord. Father, I ask that You forgive us of every sin we have committed against You, both known and unknown. Forgive us for offending You, Father, and acting as though You do not see and know our sin. Forgive us, Lord, for misrepresenting You. Forgive us for not being more conscious of You. Forgive us, Father, for carrying You into situations where You should not have been. Forgive us, O God, for not submitting to Your correction and receiving it as Your unwavering love. Draw us Lord to a place of true repentance so we can be restored back to our right place in You. Help us, Father, to no longer be satisfied in expressing sorrow and guilt for our sin, but let us also make a conscious choice for change: a change of heart and mind. **Philippians 2:5 (KJV)** states, ***"Let this mind be in you, which was also in Christ***

Jesus." Help us Lord to have the mindset You have concerning sin and repentance. Let us submit to your discipline so we can yield the peaceful fruit of righteousness. Father, let us not be a people who continue to be indifferent to Your repeated call to repentance and restoration. May we submit to Your will, Your way, Your instruction, and Your correction so we can continue to be fashioned in the image of You.

In Jesus name I pray, Amen.

PASTOR KIMBERLY VINES-WEATHERS

Pastor Kimberly Vines-Weathers, a native of Hampton, Virginia, is the eldest of three daughters born to the parents of Dr. Willie C. Vines and Decorious Vines. Educated at James Madison University, Pastor Kimberly received her Bachelor's of Science degree in Mathematics. She has also obtained her Master's of Science in Information Technology degree from the University of Maryland. She resides in Upper Marlboro, Maryland with her husband of seventeen (17) years, Apostle Timothy Weathers, and their two (2) sons. Pastor Kimberly is an anointed woman of God who loves the Lord and has a loving and caring heart for God's people. With a vision of *"Taking the Gospel to the Nations"*alongside her husband, Pastor Kimberly partners in ministry with him at RHEMA International Ministries, an apostolic and prophetic house, located in Upper Marlboro, Maryland. She travels speaking at churches, conferences, and retreats proclaiming the uncompromising Word of the Lord while also calling God's people into a true and deeper relationship with Him.

An additional ministry highlight includes her participation in the Prophetic Intercessors Council of an Empowered People (P.I.C.E.P.), a council of Intercessors joined together throughout the Washington-Metropolitan D.C. area to ignite a massive prayer movement and to intercede on behalf of the land. It is Pastor Kimberly's desire to see God's people healed, delivered, and set free to minister in the true purpose, authority, and calling placed in them by our Lord and Savior, Jesus Christ when He said, *"Let us make man in our image, after our likeness: and let them have dominion..."*

CHAPTER 2

And Its' Just Life

"For godly sorrow produces repentance leading to salvation, not to be regretted; but the sorrow of the world produces death." (II Corinthians 7:10 New King James Version NKJV).

What does it mean to repent? Does pride keep us from true repentance? The Merriam-Webster dictionary defines repentance[6] as to turn from sin and dedicate oneself to the amendment of one's life; to feel regret, conviction; to change one's mind. The things that come to my mind when we talk about true repentance are humility, Godly sorrow, and changes in one's mindset in a biblical sense conforming to the ways of Christ. It is important as followers of Christ, that we have a repented lifestyle, acknowledging that we have not arrived at such a place called perfect. In this lifetime, so many things will cause one to repent such as the afflictions or infirmities, distress to our finances, loss of a loved one, divorce, or simply making bad choices in life. The truth of the matter is if we live in this mortal body long enough we will experience the good, bad, or ugly circumstances of life. For however long the journey is, we all have our test to pass in life. Life is about making choices. The choices are life or death.

The Bible explicitly states for us to choose life. However, there are times we believe that we are choosing life. However, it may not be the life that our Lord and Savior died on the cross for us to have. There are times we feel that we are our own destiny makers. This is true to a certain degree if we are following the destiny that God have predestined for us from the foundation of the world. We should realize there are patterns of life that we must follow as followers of Christ. However, the pressures of this life may cause us to sometimes be tempted in our flesh (souls' desires) and disregard the patterns of Christ Jesus. We begin to rationalize our decision by way of the flesh instead of the Spirit of God. We struggle with the strongholds of our mind and we compromise. The end result is that we have become lured in by the enemy, the devil. When our flesh guides our decisions, there is a price to pay. The Bible states in **James 1:14-15 NKJV**, *"but each one is tempted when he is drawn away by his own desires and enticed. Then when desire is conceived, it gives birth to sin, when it is full-grown, brings forth death."* Life is so full of what ifs and why not that it causes us to become victims of our own bad decisions which causes us complications in life however *"... thanks be unto God, who always leads us in triumph in Christ..."* (**II Corinthians. 2:14 NKJV**). God is faithful to those who trust in Him. Our minds are sometimes so focused on the negativities of life that we are reluctant to see that it is such a privilege to watch God manifest His promises concerning our difficult situations. When we include God in our difficult situations or any situation should I say, we are demonstrating that we need God. He is Omnipresent, which means present everywhere at once. He already knows that we would mess things up, that is what we usually do when we don't include

God in our everyday issues. He is Omniscient and He knows all things. There is nothing too hard for God because He is Omnipotent. He is all- powerful and able to do whatever He wants.

So what does it means to repent? As I said previously, we know repentance means to change one's mindset. The mindset needs to be renewed according to the Word of God. We have to purposely realign our thinking as to living a life as Jesus Christ has shown in the Bible. True repentance does not simply mean to stop doing a thing because you may get caught or you know it is wrong. True repentance does not mean that you stop because your character might be assassinated. It means you change because you know it grieves the Holy Spirit and you want to please God.

We people of God so dearly want to live holy and an acceptable life in the sight of God. This is our reasonable service to Him however; there are times when we fail to do so. The flesh is something that we have to speak to daily. It is an enemy called the devil out here seeking daily how he can cause us to be entrapped by him and his demons. He tries to lure us in by sending suggestions into our minds. We think came from us but those suggestions are from him. We need to pray over our minds daily asking God to renew our minds and purify our hearts. I thank God for His grace and mercy because it is made readily available to us. Does pride keep us from true repentance? The Bible says, *"If I must boast, I will boast in the things which concern mine infirmity."* **(II Corinthians 11:30 NKJV)**.

The scripture reminds me of the grace of God. Through all our difficulties in life, God has graced us to go through it, not only to go through it but also to obtain the victory in that situation.

I remember when I hosted a prayer conference called the "Bind the Strongman." I encountered so much warfare that it appeared to be a dream. The warfare that I suffered was because I allowed the devil to lure me. This was because of pride and what seemed right in my own eyes. I did not allow God to fight my battle. I went into the devil's battleground armed but without instructions from God. This is just as dangerous as being unarmed. However, because of God's continued grace and mercy, He kept me. I had to repent and stay before the Father in prayer just to get through that situation. I thank God that the Holy Spirit guided me through that issue. I was able to continue my assignment with the prayer conference. It was an awesome conference and to God be all the glory.

If we as Christians do not live a repented life totally submitted to the ways of God then how can we truly be effective in the kingdom of God? The Bible says to, so let our light shine before men. If we are not living a life of holiness for others to see what would draw the unsaved to our Jesus? What would make them even interested in Him? We have to stay connected to God. The only ways that we can do that is not through religion but through relationship. We must have a prayer life. We have to have constant communication with Him. It is more listening to Him than doing all the talking.

I remember when I first really received the Holy Spirit. It was such an awesome experience. I think back to my childhood days; I was bought up in church all my life. I was baptized at a young age and confessed Jesus as Lord early. I did all the religious acts expected of a child of God. However throughout my years in life, I was, only a Sunday saint should I say. On Monday, I was that same devil with a filthy mouth and a quick temper.

I believe in some instances, people probably did not believe that I knew God at all. I was just angry all of the time. I did not even understand what was wrong with me until later on in life. I had a great deal of painful experiences in life. I lived in a fantasy world during my childhood to block out pain and disappointment. I never really knew what love was nor can I remember it ever being verbal express to me as a child. I struggled with trusting anyone. I carried all that baggage into my adult life. I was out of control.

As I mentioned before, I knew about Him but having a relationship with Him was entirely different. I knew how to pray, my Father has been a preacher ever since I was a young girl. I would listen to how he prayed, thanking Jesus first for all things. My parents are divorced and when I visited him, we stayed in church. When I was at home with my Mother, Sunday school, and church was not an option. When I was growing up church seems spooky. I was afraid as I watched people fall out and spoke in tongues. I did not understand nor was I interested. I liked the good music. Sometimes enjoyed the word when I felt it related to whatever situation I was going through at that particular time. However, I can confess that I knew not the Lord.

I am here today to let you know that there is delivering power in the Blood of Jesus! I guess the Lord had His set time for my life and my deliverance. It was not until I lost something that meant so much to me that I really came to the Lord in my adult life. See, I don't have the story that I was saved all my life. My story is that I thought I was saved all my life. My world came crashing down in one giant swoop. I lost my baby, my husband left me, my mother was diagnosed with colon cancer, and my father fell into a diabetic coma. This is just some of the things that were going on in my life at that time. There were other tormenting demons that came along. I nearly lost my mind…but God! God healed my parents but I was angry with God over the loss of my baby. I said to others "I will not pray." My heart was hardened. How many of us know that the prayers of a righteous man have much power? My parents and church family prayed many prayers for me.

While I was in that season of isolating myself from God, all kinds of mysterious things began to happen. I could not explain and if I chose to mention in this writing some may question my sanity but God began to deal with me. God began to move in my life intimately. Suddenly one day I found myself so broken in such a way that I totally surrendered to God. I repented for all I ever done. I had a thirst and hunger for Him like never before. I wanted to do nothing but, pray because I found joy in prayer. I found strength and hope again in prayer. I would just pray all the time and read the Bible repeatedly. I just wanted to know about this Jesus that had given me so much joy and strength in His presence. I found myself entering into that secret place with God. I watched Him use me prophetically in a way that I did not understand. I began to see things before they happened. I knew things that I had no humanly way of knowing. I encountered many demonic attacks as well. When I tried to tell people about them, some thought I was crazy. God began to put people in my path that understood what was going on with me. This was to let me know that I was not crazy but just was in a season of training. God has been training me ever since.

Life is like basic training in the military; you pass, fail, or are recycled. In this life as we struggle in our fleshly garments, we will find that the walk with Christ is not always an easy one. Of course, we made a decision to follow Christ when we confess with our mouths and believe with our hearts that Jesus is Lord. However, there are some tests specifically with our names on them. We can pass them or we can fail them and be recycled. I don't like being recycled because I have been recycled many times. In the basic training, you must prove that you are able to pass tests and it is the same as with living for Christ.

Our relationship with our Lord and Savior Jesus Christ must be established. We have to conform our ways to the ways of Christ. The way we know Him is through His Word, prayer, fasting and working towards living a life that is pleasing in God's sight. Our minds to be renew daily with supplication and prayer. We must make a serious sacrifice to time to spend time with the Father so that He can wash away the impurities of yesterday and prepare us for today. There is an enemy waiting to bombard us constantly with junk trying to take our focus. He will come forcefully attacking our finances, health, marriages, and families. He will also come subtly through gossip, little lies, jealousy, strife, and all those other demonic spirits that are waiting to gain access. The enemy will always try to find something to cause us to compromise our walk with God. The Bible says to resist the devil and he will flee. We have to be on watch as good soldiers knowing that the enemy has a plan to gain access in our lives. We must protect the anointing on our lives by holding on to the Christ that within us by demonstrating His ways.

It is so crucial that we live a prayerful and repented lifestyle like never before because these days before us are evil. We need the

Spirit of God to lead and guide us as we go on to be the light that so shine before men.

PRAYER

Father God in the name of Jesus, I ask You to use this chapter to minister to Your readers. I pray that the readers will be edified and this be a word in season. Father, I plead the blood of Jesus over Your people. I pray that You will cover and keep them according to Psalms 91. I pray that deliverance continues to be our portion as we walk it out each and every day. I decree healing over Your people, healing to their minds, healing to their bodies, healing to their families, and healing to their finances. I come against the assignment of the enemy against Your people with the Blood of Jesus and I decree over them that no weapon formed against them shall prosper. I speak to the dry bones in their lives and command them to live. I say live in the name of Jesus by the power and the authority of God, blessings flow, blessings flow! I thank You Lord for doing it, in Jesus mighty name I pray, Amen.

PROPHETESS JENIFER CLARK

Jenifer Clark is a wife, mother, grandmother and a prophet of the Most High God. She was ordained as an evangelist in 2004. She was affirmed as a prophet in 2007 and ordained into the Office of Prophet in 2008. Jenifer is a Prophetic Intercessor and prayer is her passion. Her mandate is to train and connect with Intercessors to take prayer across the Nations. She is the Visionary of Called2Pray International Ministries. She is a Servant Leader and she assists several ministries and acknowledges that she is called to many. Her Apostolic Covering is Apostle Marc Richardson of Kingdom City International Churches. Her prophetic mentor and teacher is Bishop RS Walker, Founder of Another Touch of Glory Ministries and Heritage Church International.

Jenifer acknowledges and is grateful for the other awesome leaders that made impartations in her life such as Apostle Vincent Wyche, Apostle Monica Sweeney, Apostle Sharon Peace and of course, Overseer Trena Stephenson who helped her from the very beginning.

She serves as a board member on Word of Peace Ministries, Faith Worship Center, Called2Pray International Ministries, and Christian

Fundamentalist Internal Revenue Employees.

Jenifer served in the US Army Reserves for 15 years. She is a retired corrections officer from the Virginia Department of Corrections and currently works for the United States Treasury Department. She completed the management and leadership curriculum at Bluefield College and the project management curriculum from Villanova University. She has many accomplishments and she gives God all the glory for what He has done in her life and most importantly she firmly believes, "It's All About Him."

CHAPTER 3

True Repentance

What is True repentance? This is a very broadsided question I asked myself when writing this chapter for Daughters of Distinction. I have listed a great deal of information on repentance in the Bible. I found it to be very rewarding and refreshing. I asked the Lord to give me the right words to share. You will find them here.

WHAT IS REPENTANCE ?

Repentance is acknowledging your sin. According to Revelations 3:3 "**Remember what you were taught. Hold to those things and repent.**" (**Revelations 3:3 New International Version NIV**). "**The Lord knows those who are his,**" and "**everyone who confesses the name of the Lord must turn away from wickedness.**" (**II Timothy 2:19 NIV**). Why should we repent? "When at first we think of the word "repent or perish," it may seem a little harsh. However, as we turn, we see that it is an incredible gift to have something to turn to. If it were not for God's love, we would all perish. However, the grace of our Lord and Savior Jesus Christ has given us as Christians the right to a full life. In true repentance, we know and recognize that God is willing and able to forgive our sin. People do not want to hear the word Repent.

People in hell wish they could hear it just one more time! Now is the time to repent people! Please remember the time is NOW! Repentance of the mind and the heart leads to salvation and consists of three steps:

STEP 1 – RECOGNIZE YOUR GUILT

"The idea here is that we understand who we are and where we stand before God. 1 John 1:8 tells us that "*if we say that we have no sin, we deceive ourselves, and the truth is not in us.*" While Romans 6:23 tells us the "*wages of sin is death.*" The first step in repenting involves understanding that we are sinners and stand under God's judgment.[7]

STEP 2 – TRUST THAT GOD WILL FORGIVE YOU

David wrote many of the Psalms, and he was certainly one man very familiar with sexual sin and spiritual warfare. Let us look at Psalm 51, which is one of my favorites. Verses 1-13 are an excellent prayer that we can pray on a daily basis. David wrote it after the Prophet Nathan confronted David with his sin of adultery. In Psalm 51 David wrote, "Have mercy on me, O God, according to your unfailing love; according to your great compassion blot out my transgressions."[8] Do you think if God could forgive David of adultery and murder that he can't also forgive you of drug addictions, adultery, lust, sexual sin, just to name a few? Repentance is not only acknowledging our sin, it is also recognizing that God is willing and able to forgive our sin. Hebrews 8:12 promises that God will *"forgive our wickedness and will remember our sins no more* **(NIV)**." The second step in repenting involves believing that God will forgive us.

STEP 3 – TURN FROM SIN, TO GOD

Once we realize that we stand before God guilty of sin, and that He is willing to forgive us, we must then come to Him to receive that forgiveness. We come to God the Father though Jesus Christ, who is God the Son. John 3:16 declares that *"God so loved the world that He gave His only begotten Son, that whoever believes in Him should not perish but have everlasting life."* I John 4:10 tells us that Christ is *"the propitiation [or payment] for our sins."* Because Christ paid for our sins, Romans 3:24 tells us that we have been "justified freely" through Him, and we now stand before God innocent. The final step in repenting involves calling on Christ to save us from the penalty of sin. Acts 2:21 promises that *"whoever calls on the name of the Lord shall be saved."* Once we have repented and come to Christ for forgiveness Ephesians 2:19 tell us we are *"no longer foreigners and aliens, but fellow citizens with God's people and members of God's household."*[9]

We must feel Godly sorrow. I once was addicted to drugs and alcohol. I literally struggled with this addiction for years. I asked God to heal my body from this horrible affliction and He did. God is amazing. He healed me took me from the depths of hell and set my feet on solid ground. He allowed me to go back in the military and start a new life. We must confess to God. I asked God to heal me I knew that the demons that I was struggling with were much larger than me. I turned it over to the Lord and He worked it out.

Ask for forgiveness. I asked God to forgive me for abusing my body using drugs and alcohol. I also asked Him to forgive me for all the pain I caused my loved ones during the most difficult time of my life. I was very sincere. I wanted help. I knew He was the only one who could rectify the problems caused by sin. I stopped using drugs found me a bible believing church and started to study the word of God. I read and studied God's Word. I know that He can and will supply all my needs. God will never forsake us. He said in His word. By doing this we receive forgiveness.

How are we forgiven if we sin? We now know that we all have sinned or come short. What is sin the word sin translates from a Greek word, which means missing the mark. Notice how it is used in Scripture *"For all have sinned and come short of the glory..."* (Romans 3:23 KJV). What can we do when we sin to be forgiven? I John 1:9 states, *"If we confess our sins. (God) is faithful and just and will forgive our sins and purify us from all unrighteousness."* (I John 1:9 NIV). *"⁶Seek the Lord while he may be found; call on him while he is near. ⁷Let the wicked forsake his way and the evil man his thoughts. Let him turn to the Lord, and he will have mercy on him, and to our God, for he will freely pardon."* (Isaiah 55:6-7 NIV). *"Are you, perhaps, misinterpreting God's generosity and patient mercy towards you as weakness on his part? Don't you realize that God's kindness is meant to lead you to repentance?"* (Romans 2:4 J.B Phillips New Testament PHI). *"In the past God overlooked such ignorance, but now he commands all people everywhere to repent."* (Acts 17:30 NIV). *"My brothers, if any of you should wander away from the truth and another should turn him back on to the right path, then the latter may be sure that in turning a man back from his wandering course he has rescued a soul from death, and in so doing will "cover a multitude of sins."* James 5:19-20 PHI).

According to the word of God, this comes from the bible *"For God so loved the world that he gave his one and only son. That whoever believes in him shall not perish but have everlasting life."* **(John 3:16 NIV)**. We know that *"the thief comes only to steal kill and destroy. I (Jesus) have come that you may have life and have it to the fullest."* **(John 10:10 NIV)**. This tells us that the reason Jesus came was because the thief wanted to kill and destroy us. However, Jesus came so we could have a full an abundant life.

"For all have sinned and fall short of the glory of God" **(Romans 3:23 KJV)**. *"For the wages of sin is death, but the gift of God is eternal life in Christ Jesus our Lord"* **(Romans 6:23 KJV)**. This lets us know how many have sinned. It clearly states all have sinned and the wages of sin according to Romans 3:23 & 6:23 is death. *"Jesus said I am the way and the truth and the life. No one comes to the Father except by me"* **(John 14:6 KJV)**. This tells us know that no one can come by the Father except through Jesus Christ.

"But God demonstrates His own love for us in this." **(Romans 5:8 NIV)**. *"³For what I received I passed on to you that as of first importance; that Christ died for our sins according to scriptures For what I received I passed on to you ⁴that he was buried, that he arose on the third day according to the scriptures, ⁵and that he appeared to Peter, and to the twelve disciples. ⁶After that he appeared to more than five hundred of the brothers at the same time, most of who are still living, though some have fallen asleep. Then he appeared to James, then to all the apostles, and last of all he appeared*

to me also, as one abnormally born" **(I Corinthians 15:3-6 NIV)**. We must receive Jesus as our Lord and Savior. *"Yet to all who received him, to those who believed in his name, he gave the right to become children of God"* **(John 1:12 NIV)**. This tells us we must receive Him and believe in His name to become children of God. God chooses to save us by faith not by works. *"8For it is by grace you have been saved, and this is not from yourselves. It is a gift of God 9not by works, so that no one can boast."* **(Ephesians 2:8-9 NIV)**. This tells us it is not our words but our faith that is important to God. We must trust Christ to forgive us for our sins. He promised He would in His word. Have you personally received Christ as your Lord and Savior, and trusted Him to forgive you of your sins? If not and would like to, you can make this important decision right now. It is the best decision you could ever make in your life. Do this right now! Just say, "Dear, Lord Jesus I confess that I have sinned against You and need Your forgiveness. Thank You for dying on the cross in my place for my sins. I receive You into my life and trust in You alone as my Savior and God. In Your name, I pray. Amen. In return for this, you are given eternal life and this is the testimony: *"God has given us eternal life and this life is in His son. He who has Jesus has life. I write these things to you who believe in the name of the Son of God as that you may know you have eternal life"* **(I John 5:11-13 NIV)**.

We now know God considers us all sinners. *"For all have sinned and come short of the glory of God"* **(Romans 3:23 KJV)**. *"Repent, then, and <u>turn to</u> God, so that your sins may* be wiped out, that times of refreshing may come from the Lord." (Acts 3:19 NIV). *"Let us fix our eyes on Jesus, the author and finisher of our faith.* (Hebrews 12:2 NIV).*[10]* *"Godly sorrow produces repentance leading to salvation..."* **(II Corinthians 7:10 NKJV)**. Since Christ paid for our sins, **Romans 3:24** tells us that we have been "justified freely" through Him, and we now stand before God innocent. The final step in repenting involves calling on Christ to save us from the penalty of sin. Acts 2:21 promises that *"whoever calls on the name of the Lord shall be saved."* **(Acts 2:21 NKJV)**. Once we have repented and come to Christ for forgiveness Ephesians 2:19 tell us we are *"no longer foreigners and aliens, but fellow citizens with God's people and members of God's household."* **(Ephesians 2:19 NIV)**.

PRAYER

Dear Lord, all honor, and glory go to you my Jehovah Jireh, my Daddy, my everlasting Father. I love You! I thank You I humbly come before You in the precious name of Jesus! I pray that You will not remember the sins of my youth, or of my past nor my transgressions. Please think of me according to Your mercy and for Your goodness sake, O LORD. Lord I turn from all of those sins that I committed and I ask for Your help in washing the memories and thoughts of those sin's completely from my mind. Please restore me to faithful obedience to Your Word, and fill me with Your Holy Spirit anew, so that I may keep your commands all the days of my life." (Based on Psalm 25:7)

Lord Jesus, my wonderful savior. You are my counselor of peace. I invite You into my heart anew today, and I ask forgiveness for all of my sin. Jesus, thank You for dying on the cross for my sins. And for forgiving me of my sins through Your bloodshed for me on the cross. Please take away all the sinful "old things" in my heart that defile me, especially whatever it is I'm struggling with today. Replace them with the "good things" that You desire to grow in to my life. Please wash away all the sinful crud and tendencies toward evil. Replace them with a hunger and thirst for Your righteousness.

I need Your help, Father I know I cannot do this on my own. Lord God as I live this new life in Christ, please send Your Holy Spirit afresh into my life to help, heal, lead, and transform me. Lord I ask these blessings in the wonderful name of Jesus Christ I pray. Amen. (Refer to Mark 7:21-23 & 2 Corinthians 5:17).

Now is the time to repent. Let go of these worldly things for our Father has promised a great reward for those who diligently seek him with all their heart and soul. Repent and be saved from the depth of hell. Trust Jesus, He will never leave you or forsake you. He is Alpha and Omega the beginning and the end. He is our source the connection to the Father. As for me, I cannot live my life without Him. He has been so good to me. I will trust Him the rest of my days. We can all be renewed through repentance. I want to share with you the Prayer of Repentance:

We repent, O God most merciful; for all our sins;
for every thought that was false or unjust or unclean;
for every word spoken, that ought not to have been spoken;
for every deed done that ought not to have been done.
We repent for every deed and word and thought inspired by
selfishness and for every deed and word and thought inspired by
hatred.

We repent most specially for every lustful thought and every lustful action; for every lie; for all hypocrisy; for every promise given but not fulfilled and for all slander and backbiting. Most specially also, we repent for every action that has brought ruin to others; for every word and deed that has given others pain; and for every wish, that pain should befall others. In your unbounded mercy, we ask you to forgive us, O God, for all these sins committed by us, and to forgive us for our constant failures to think, speak, and act according to your will.[11]

So now that I have given you my take on repentance what is yours? God wants you to repent so he can restore you for all seeking, to be refreshed and restored. Repent today!

VERNESSA BLACKWELL

Vernessa R. Blackwell is a native of Waldorf, Maryland. She enlisted in the Army in 1994 and completed overseas tours to include Operation Iraqi Freedom. She is a graduate of Strayer University.

Vernessa Blackwell has served in her current assignment as the S1- Operations NCO since December 2011. Among her military awards and decorations are Army Commendation (fourth award), Joint Service Commendation Medal (second Award), Army Achievement Medal (second Award), Noncommissioned Officers Development ribbon with numeral (2) National Defense Medal with Iraqi Campaign Badge.

Staff Sergeant Vernessa Blackwell is divorced and the proud mother of 2 daughters, Darkema and Takia and seven wonderful grandchildren Tyquan, Kemonte, Khyeema, Davonte, Khalil, Terrence, and Kamille. Vernessa came to know Christ in 1985. She is a member of Sanctuary of Kingdom Square.

She is the proud owner of Anointed Affairs Weddings and Events founded in 1997.

CHAPTER 4

A Changed Life and the Love of Our Savior

Repentance, referring to a complete turn from self to God, was the key note of the preaching of John the Baptist, who was the forerunner to announce the coming of Jesus Christ. A note of urgency is attached to the message, the "kingdom of heaven has come near! **(Matthew 3:2)**. Those who were prepared to make such a reorientation of their lives demonstrated that by being baptized **(Mark 1:4)**. This complete redirection of their lives was to be demonstrated by profound changes in lifestyle and relationships **(Luke 3:8-14)**.

SINNER CALLED TO REPENTANCE

The emphasis upon a total life change continues in the ministry of Jesus. The message of repentance was at the heart of His preaching **(Mark 1:15)**. When describing the focus of His mission, Jesus said, *"I have not come to call the righteous, but sinners to repentance."* **(Luke 5:32 KJV)**.

Healthy people do not need a doctor – the physician's waiting room is filled with sick people. They recognize their need and come to the one who can make them well. The religious leaders of that day were appalled that Jesus ate with sinners and outcast. The religious leaders love of principle and position made them feel that they were above association with prostitutes, harlots, and sinners. However, Jesus further explained His mission that He had come to call sinners to turn from their sins, not to spend His time with those who think they are already good enough. Jesus was saying that I am here to call sinners to turn from their sins. These are the people who realize that they need Jesus, the Great Physician, who healed people of physical illnesses, but He knew that all people are spiritually sick and in need of salvation.

SALVATION TO THE WORLD

"God so loved the world that he gave his only begotten Son, that whosoever believeth in him should not perish, but have everlasting life." **(John 3:16).**

The entire gospel comes to a focus in this verse. God's love is not just to a certain group of individuals. It is offered to the world. God's love is not static or self-centered; it reaches out and draws in others. Here God's action defined the pattern of true love, the basis for all love relationships. When you love someone, you are willing to sacrifice dearly for that person. Sacrificial is also practical in seeking ways to meet the needs of those who are loved. In God's case, that love was infinitely practical; since it set out to rescue those who had no hope of rescuing themselves. God paid dearly to save us. He gave His son, the highest ransom He could pay.

This offer is made to everyone who believes. To believe is more than intellectual agreement that Jesus is God. It means putting our trust and confidence in Him that He alone can save us. It is to put Christ in charge of our present plans and eternal destiny. Believing is both trusting His words as reliable and relying on Him for the power to change.

Jesus accepted our punishment and paid the price for our sins so that we would not perish. Perish does not mean physical death, for we all will eventually die. Here it is refers to eternity apart from God. Those who believe will receive the alternative, the new life that Jesus bought for us – eternal life with God.

The call to repentance is a call to absolute surrender to the purposes of God and to live in this awareness. This radical turning to God required all people: Unless you repent, you will all perish **(Luke 13:3)**. Those who had witnessed the ministry of Jesus, the reality of God, and His claims on their lives faced serious jeopardy if they failed to repent. Jesus warned of serious consequences for those where His ministry had been rejected. For the one sinner who repents there is great joy in heaven **(Luke 15:7)**. In His final words to the disciples, Jesus demanded that the same message of repentance He had preached would be preached to all nations.

True repentance is a fundamental and thorough change in the hearts of men from sin and toward God. Although faith alone is the condition for salvation **(Ephesians 2:8-10; Acts 16:31)**, repentance is bound up with faith and inseparable from it. Since without some measure of faith no one *can truly repent*, and repentance never attains to its deepest character until the sinner realizes through saving faith how great is the grace of God against whom he has sinned. On the other hand, there can be no saving faith without *true* repentance. Saving faith is faith in Jesus Christ is God's requirement for receiving His gift of salvation.

Repentance contains as essential elements the following:
 A genuine sorrow toward God on account of sin **(II Corinthians 7:9, 10, Matthew 5:3, 4; Psalm51)**.

 Many people are sorry only for the effects of their sins or for being caught. Sorrow without repentance literally means "the sorrow of the world." When people don't channel their grief over their behavior into life-changing actions, it is unproductive grief. It leads to self-pity. Godly sorrow is practical and action-oriented. When a person realizes that he or she has done wrong, that person should not only regret the error but also turn back to God. Only God can empower people to change their ways. Only God can save people from the way sin imprisons them and paralyzes them. Only God can help us turn away from sin and seek salvation.

 Comparing the stories of Peter and Judas, both handled the events surrounding the death of Jesus in a wrong way. Judas brazenly betrayed Jesus with a kiss **(Mark 14:43-46)** Peter denied knowing Jesus three different times **(John 18:15-27)**. Both were overcome with grief over their actions **(Matthew 26:75; 27:3)**. Although Peter was distraught, he had the humility and the courage to admit his failure, reform his behavior, and rededicate his life to the cause of Jesus **(John 21:15-19)**.

 In contrast, Judas let his remorse eat at his soul. Eventually overcome by guilt, he committed suicide. Judas wasn't able to learn from his sin and repent. He didn't submit his sins to Christ and beg to be forgiven.

He was too proud to cry out for salvation, so his stubbornness led to him taking his own life.

THE SPIRIT OF THE SON DWELLS IN THE BELIEVER

"Because you are sons, God sent forth the spirit of His Son into our hearts, the Spirit who calls out, "Abba Father." **(Galatians 4:6)**. The same Spirit (the Holy Spirit) that dwelled and still dwells in the Son becomes the life of the believer. This means that we become sons, that is God's Children, part of God's family. All believers, from the moment they accept Jesus Christ, as the Forgiver of their sins and Leader of their lives, have the Holy Spirit living in them (Romans 8:9). One of the Holy Spirit's tasks is to create in God's children a feeling of love relating to parents and family that causes them to know God as their Father. The term, "Abba" is Aramaic term meaning "Father." It was the term Jesus used when referring to His Heavenly Father. Christ used this term in his prayer in Mark 14:36. The combining of the Aramaic term "Abba" with the Greek term for Father (pater) expresses the depth of intimacy, warmth and confidence by which the Holy Spirit helps us to relate to and cry out to God in prayer (Romans 8:15).

MY SOUL THIRST FOR GOD

"¹As the deer pants for the streams of water, so my soul pants for you, O God. ²My soul thirsts for God for the living God." **(Psalm 42:1-2 NIV)**.

As water is essential for physical life, so God and His presence are essential for our spiritual life and complete satisfaction and wholeness in all areas of life. Those who truly trust God will hunger and thirst for a deeper relationship with Him and for His favor and supernatural activity in their lives.

Believers must avoid becoming distracted by the circumstances of life, including worries, needs, successes, attractions, and pleasures. These things can choke out our hunger and thirst for God. They can also rob us of the desire and discipline needed to pursue a deeper relationship with God though His word and through prayer.

True believers will hunger and thirst for God and His grace, blessing and supernatural activity in their lives. To stop thirsting for God is to die spiritually, thus we must not allow anything to diminish our intense desire for the things of God. Beware of the cares of this world, the pursuit of earthly things, and the pleasures that choke out hunger and thirst for God and the desire to seek His face in prayer. We should pray that our desire for God's presence might become deeper and stronger within us and gives us a spiritual thirst like a deer that "pants for streams of water" in times of drought and along with a greater passion to see Christ's purposes fulfilled on earth.

MY PRAYER

Heavenly Father,

I come before You today, with a heart of repentance asking that You forgive me of all my sins that I have committed knowingly and unknowingly, and cleanse me with the blood of Your dear son Jesus Christ. According to I John 1:9, your word says, "If I confess my sins you are faithful and just to forgive my sins and to cleanse me of all unrighteousness." I receive Your forgiveness and I believed that I am cleansed by the blood of the lamb. I ask that Your presence will continuously be upon me and that the love of Your dear son Jesus Christ continues to shine in my heart to touch persons that have never experienced the love of Christ. Father I pray that all the body of believers, will continue to walk in the love of Christ and be examples for the world to experience and see the love of your dear son manifest visually through us. Father, I pray that we yearn for a deeper relationship with You so that the Spirit of Your dear son will manifest the sacrificial love in our lives that can be shown toward mankind so that You will get the glory with our lives, in Jesus name I pray. I love you Father, Amen.

REVEREND JACQUELINE ADAMS COOK

Reverend Jacqueline Adams Cook is the only child born to the late Mr. & Mrs. John Julian and Lila Mae Adams. She is a graduate of American University, Washington, D.C. with a Bachelor of Science in Accounting. She has also received a Bachelor of Science in Christian Counseling, a Master of Theological Studies, and a Master of  Divinity Degree from the National Bible College and Seminary in Fort Washington, Maryland. She is continuing to pursue her studies toward a Doctorate of Ministry.

Reverend Cook has served and worked in the church since she was a little girl. Her grandmother would often tell her stories of how even at the ages of 3 and 4 years old; she would get happy and shout, just like her grandmother. As a child, she gave her life to the Lord. Reverend Cook believes that the elders working with the youth when she was a child, greatly contributed to her knowledge and desire to work with children. Her Christian service has included singing with the Sincere Gospel Singers and the Voices of Mt. Zion; working with children of all ages at Mt Zion Baptist Church and with H. J. Hines Ministries, where she served as Secretary of the Board for about 10 years.

Reverend Cook is currently an Associate Minister at Mt Zion Baptist Church, under the leadership of the Pastor, Reverend Dr. John W. Davis. She continues to teach, preach, and work with the Mt. Zion Baptist Church Prayer Army and provide Pastoral Counseling, under the direction of Pastor John W. Davis. In addition to her current duties, Reverend Cook previously served as Youth Director and Youth Minister of the Youth and Young Adult Department for several years. God has blessed Reverend Cook with her husband, Herman Sr.; two sons, Herman Jr. and Derrick; and one grandchild, Chase Elijah.

CHAPTER 5

So, What Are You Lookin' At?

Have you ever noticed how many people get plowed down on the side of the road by passing motorists? The evening news and newspapers are full of these reports. Changing a flat tire, working under the hood of a car, or even being a police officer issuing a citation can be a life-threatening situation. While the majority of these incidents are not intentional, a stop on the shoulder of the road can be perilous. What is going on? Well, it has been shown that whatever a driver has his eyes focused on is the direction he will unconsciously steer his vehicle. Ruling out people that are clearly not visible, when a driver focuses his attention on what's happening on the roadside, everyone had better watch out because that is where the car will be going too! The same principle applies to our lives. Whatever we focus on will be the direction our life will take. So I ask a question --- what are *you* looking at?

Mankind's natural focus is on sin. Sin is wrongful actions that break the laws of God.[12] Unfortunately, man feels comfortable with sin, he delights in sin, and he even pursues sin. Why? Sin is the nature of mankind. The Word of God tells us that man was born in sin and shaped in iniquity **(Romans 5:12-19)**. If man was born and shaped in sin, then in his natural state of mind, he has no regard for the things of God **(Romans 8:5-8)**. Therefore, his life will go the way he's looking, in the direction of sin.

You have probably heard the story of the woman that brought home a snake. The snake's skin had such stunning colors and unique designs on it, that she wanted him for a pet. Taking him home, she fed him, gave him plenty of room to move about, and she made life very comfortable for the snake. She constantly gazed upon him, always marveling at how beautiful he was. One day, out of the blue, the snake bit her! As the poisonous venom coursed quickly through her bloodstream, she weakly looked at the snake and asked him why he had bitten her. She had done everything for him, she made his life easy, and she loved him. Why had he done such a horrible thing? The snake looked at her and said, "You knew what I was when you brought me home." Quite frankly, he did not understand why the woman was so shocked. After all, he was a snake. So, his final reply to the dying woman was, "That's what I do."

It didn't matter how beautiful the snake was, how comfortable he was, or who loved him. Having the nature of a snake caused him to act like a snake, such is our "old" man. He was shaped in sin and it causes us to operate according to that nature. It is our sinful nature that causes us to be separated from God **(Isaiah 59:2)**. When we look at the state of the world, not just today, but back through time, we often shake our heads and think how did it get this *bad*! It's not that God is not caring, or that God doesn't love us. It got this bad because man was acting in his sin nature. God longs to be able to fully act as the Father of His Creation for all who will receive Him. However, He cannot be associated with sin in any form because it's not His nature. This very scripture also lets us know that God cannot even hear our prayers as long as there is unconfessed sin in our lives. Consequently, there is a monumental divide between God and us. But, hold on! The fabulous news is that God sent His Son Jesus to bridge the gap between God and man.

Jesus Christ died for our sins **(Romans 5:8)** and by sacrificing His life for us, we now have eternal life **(John 3:16)**. In the face of such sacrifice, the sorrow and remorse for our sins must be so great that we no longer have affection for it. Our faith should *burn* within us to follow the One responsible for giving us eternal life. In order to follow Christ, God commands in **Acts 17:30** that all men everywhere should repent.

Repentance is a term loosely used; often minimizing the fact that repentance is a *huge* undertaking! Repentance is bigger than regret and it's more than, "Oops, sorry! I'll do better next time." The word repentance is from the Hebrew term "teshubah," meaning to turn[13]Therefore to turn from one's nature to walk in a completely different direction, requires a willpower that only God can sustain.

Repentance is a state of *action* --- an act of turning from our basic nature of sin towards God's way of holiness. Just as we steer a car in the direction in which we are looking, so must we look at Christ in order to turn everything within us toward Him. Only when we look to God can we live in righteousness, oh, not by the world's standards, but with the help of the Holy Spirit, we can live to the standards God has set in His Word. To continue in sin will clearly result in man's destruction **(Ezekiel 18:30 and Romans 6:23)**.

Once we repent, or turn away from sin, what do we turn to? We must repent unto salvation. Repenting unto salvation means that the sorrow we feel for our sins is so strongly heartfelt that the pain of having sinned turns us to God, to seek eternal life with Him. We can stop doing some ungodly things but this does not mean we have repented of our sins. We may become a "good" person but still be spiritually lost. We all know good people. They are people with high morals, they do the right thing, and they are productive members of society. But, that is all they are. They do not have their eyes turned toward Heaven or their hearts turned toward God. They don't have any interest in God's plan. Good people may no longer live a life filled with sin, but they have not repented unto salvation. We must be more than a "good person." Good people focus their minds on the world, wanting to do right by society, while their souls are headed to hell because they have no interest in doing right by God. So what are *you* looking at?

Both **Luke 3:8** and **Acts 26:20** declare that along with true repentance comes a real change of behavior. Our lives should no longer resemble that of the past because God comes in and gives us a new nature. Unlike the snake in the earlier story, our nature *will* change, and we will not act like what we once were.

Positive behavior produces positive results. In spiritual terms, positive results are called fruit. When walking in an orchard, the fruit hanging from the bough of the tree identifies the type of tree it is. Similarly, the fruit of our behavior will identify who *we* are. Turning toward a righteous life will bear Godly fruit. As in Matthew **3:8**, we should produce fruit in keeping with repentance. In Ephesians **4:23-32** the Apostle Paul makes it very clear what changes of behavior should be seen in a life that has turned to God. Let's look at them:

First, with the renewing of our minds, we have a different

outlook and perspective. We know the road we will be traveling is a different one than the road we are used to. We will be a "new" man, fashioned after God, speaking truth to all men. Do not be misguided however. We will still battle the nature of that old man! The good news is that as we grow in God, and let God grow in us, when each layer of the old man is peeled away, it will uncover a person looking more and more like Christ. Beware, but don't get discouraged that the old man has many layers, and the process of changing who we are will not happen overnight. We will be evolving until we take our last breath!

Next, Paul informs us we are not to sin when we're angry. We will experience anger because we still have human emotions. However, through God's power working in us, we can control our anger and not let our anger control us. If anger takes control, we may slip into sinful actions. If we follow the guidance of the scripture, and not let the sun go down on our anger, we are provided a window of time to let go of the anger so that it will not consume us.

While we get into enough trouble on our own, we also have Satan standing on the sidelines wanting to take control of our lives once again. We should never forget how the devil is a fan of the "old" man. Picture him on the sidelines of your life, jumping up and down, yelling or sometimes whispering, "Do it! Do it!" Well, we must not let him take a stand in any area of our lives. Paul says we must not give him a place. We are governed and operate by our five senses. It is therefore important that we keep our five senses under subjection to Christ and protect what we see, feel, hear, touch, and smell, in order to keep the devil off our playing field!

Another change in behavior by being a child of God is that we don't steal. We get what we need through honest labor. Then after we have labored in order to get our provisions, we must remember that we also have an obligation to help those in need. We can never forget that we are one body leaning, depending, and supporting one another.

In case, it has not dawned on you yet, God is a Creator who absolutely loves His creation! He not only loves us, but wants us to love one another as well. Therefore, any conversation transpiring between us and others is to be that which bless and build up each other, being careful not to tear down one another.

Paul states that we are not to grieve the Holy Spirit. Think about how we do not want to disappoint our earthly parents. How much *more* should we not want to disappoint God by our actions! The Living Bible states so pointedly in verse 30 of Ephesians 4, "Remember He (the Holy Spirit) is the one who marks you to be present on that day when salvation from sin will be *complete*." That is a sobering thought as we contemplate our actions! Don't disappoint God.

The characteristics of the old nature should no longer be a part of us. Paul's list continues in that we should put away bitterness, wrath, anger, quarreling, and evil speaking. We should treat one another as God treats us; forgive others as He constantly forgives us. What love God has for us! This list shows that the old man must be put firmly behind us. In summary, true repentance is turning away from sin and turning to God. This is the action God wants to see from us. It is the big picture. However, within this large framework of repentance, some important things must take place.

One, we cannot turn to God without first acknowledging that

we are a sinner. We must know in our heart that we have sinned against God and man. We must understand who we are in order to know who we need to become. Next, we turn toward God believing Jesus Christ is the Son of God, and that He alone paid the price by dying and rising again from the dead, victorious, to redeem us from our sins.

Lastly, we must confess our sins. There is not enough time in a day to list our sins individually, but as a whole, we confess that we have sinned in thoughts, deeds, and actions. Confession should be with complete brokenness, total guilt and shame. Only then do we realize our deeds are so corrupt that we needed someone to rescue us. That person is Jesus Christ, who hung on a cross in our stead. It is that person whom we ask to come and live in our hearts. Only then are we liberated to live free from sin, having the confidence that God has forgiven us, washed us, and given us a new nature.

You may think the above paragraphs sound like the plan of salvation. It is. Having Godly sorrow for our sins and having faith in the Son of God who will restore a right relationship with the Father. This is the key to an effective prayer that will make true repentance complete until God takes us home with Him! For us to live a victorious life, we must keep our focus on things above. Christ is the only redemption from sin. So, it is *Him* whom we look to for redemption. Therefore, as we look at our

lives to see where we are, our focus should always be Christ. So, what are *you* looking at?

PRAYER FOR REPENTANCE

God, I confess all of the sins that I have committed in thought, words, and deeds. I ask forgiveness for making You sorrowful because of my acts of disobedience. I accept Jesus as my Lord and Savior and I wish to turn, with Your help, from my sinful ways and do only the things that pleases You. By Your grace, I want to walk in the ways of righteousness. I will always praise You for the love and forgiveness You have shown towards me.

Amen.

PRISCILLA HAIRSTON

Priscilla Hairston is a veteran educator, holding a Master's degree in Education, as well as being a Certified Reading Specialist, and trained Mentor Teacher. She has tailored, designed, and conducted workshops for educational institutions and school districts on how to build self-esteem in children. As a certified Professional Life Coach, as well as  Diversity Trainer with emphasis in women's issues, she is the owner of Mosaic Consulting Services.

Priscilla is a contributing author for the book entitled, "Self-Esteem & Empowerment for Women," as well as the co-author of "Meaningful Life Moments." Priscilla currently resides with her husband in northern Virginia.

CHAPTER 6

Lord, Change My Heart

Why do we have to pray to a God who knows everything about us? God, why do certain things happen? How can I change my ways and situations in my life? This was a question I always asked as a child growing up. As I grew older, I realized that prayer is the key factor to having a relationship and communicating with the Creator, our Heavenly Father. It opens the door for man to talk, hear, and most importantly, get instructions concerning our lives.

As we reflect on the Word of God, the Bible tells us in Genesis 1:27 that *"... God created man in his own image, in the image of God created he him; male and female created he them."* **(Genesis 1:27 KJV).** *"For by him (God) were all things created, that are in heaven, and that are in earth, visible and invisible, whether they be thrones, or dominions, or principalities, or powers: all things were created by him, and for him."* **(Colossians 1:16 KJV).** Merriam Webster's Collegiate Dictionary defines the word "image" as a "reproduction or imitation of the form of a person or a thing; an exact likeness.[14]" Being created in an "image" means the object is to pattern after the original model. An image should be a "tangible or visible representation."

Actions and image walk hand and hand. We must first believe in the One who created us. *"But without faith it is impossible to please and be satisfactory to Him. For whoever would come near to God must [necessarily] believe that God exists and that He is the rewarder of those who earnestly and diligently seek Him [out]."* **(Hebrews 11:6 Amplified AMP**). As we grow in God, 2 Corinthians 3:18 informs us that *"As all of us reflect the Lord's glory with faces that are not covered with veils, we are being changed into his image with ever-increasing glory. This comes from the Lord, who is the Spirit."* **(II Corinthians 3:18 GOD'S WORD).**

God never intended for man to live apart from Him. He provides instructions for each us to live by and it must begin in our heart. From the Old Testament to the New Testament, God has described His very image to us through His word. The Bible instructs us to"[14]*[Live] as children of obedience [to God]; don't conform yourselves to the evil desires [that governed you] in your former ignorance [when you did not know the requirements of the Gospel]. [15]But as the One Who called you is holy, you yourselves also be holy in all your conduct and manner of living. [16]For it is written, You shall be holy, for I am holy."* **(I Peter 1:14-16 AMP).**

In order to live as the Creator God wants us, Proverbs 3:5-6 tells us to [5]*"Lean on, trust in, and be confident in the Lord with all your heart and mind and don't rely on your own insight or understanding. [6]In all your ways know, recognize, and acknowledge Him, and He will direct and make straight and plain your paths."* **(Proverbs 3:5-6 AMP).** How do we reflect God's image? We are to pattern our lives according to His Son, Jesus Christ. He was the perfect example of the Creator. He proclaimed,

"Very truly I tell you, the Son can do nothing by himself; he can do only what he sees his Father doing, because whatever the Father does the Son also does. For the Father loves the Son and shows him all he does. Yes, and he will show him even greater works than these, so that you will be amazed." **(John 5:19-20 NIV).** Jesus identified himself with God. He reflected His image by His actions. *"...He is the exact likeness of the unseen God [the visible representation of the invisible]; He is the Firstborn of all creation."* **(Colossians 1:15 AMP).** Believing and trusting God brings us to a place of humility and surrender. Living a life of surrender allows us to desire God's will and not our own just as Jesus did, which is an image that reflects our Creator.

However, before Jesus was born, mankind made a decision to disobey God by the influence of the serpent, which yielded disobedience entering into the world. Being born from the offspring of the first man, Adam and Eve, we have all fallen into a sinful state because of whom we originate from in the flesh. The world became corrupt and that was the beginning of people seeking other images and likenesses. Disobedience begins with a thought that turns into an action. When we feed our mind anything other than the word of God, it taints our soul. Living in a world that has been structured by man often causes us to seek out our own destiny. Our hearts (our will) draw far from God. What draws our heart away from replicating God in the earth? Our selfish desires. The world is filled with images other than God. The Bible tells us that *".... in the world—the lust of the flesh [craving for sensual gratification] and the lust of the eyes [greedy longings of the mind] and the pride of life [assurance in one's own resources or in the stability of earthly things]—these don't come from the Father but are from the world [itself]."* **(I John 2:16 AMP).** In our hearts, there is a desire for physical gratification, meaning we have our own desires. We focus our eyes on those things that change and alter things our stability in God and we rest within our own accomplishments. What dictates these actions and behaviors? What we feed our minds. In order for the body to live, there are certain ingredients that are needed for the body to function: food, water, oxygen, and sleep. These ingredients produce actions in the human body. In order for plants to grow, they need to have the following in order to function: sunlight, water, soil and air. These ingredients cause something to happen, growth of a plant. When Jesus was tempted in the wilderness by Satan, He stated, *"… it has been written, Man shall not live and be upheld and sustained by bread alone, but by every word that comes forth from the mouth of God."* **(Matthew 4:4 AMP).** It is the word of God that tells us who we are, and instructs our lives.

If we are to be an image of the living God, we must be like Him through and through and He provides an opportunity for us to do it while living on earth. God has given man free will to accept His guidance and will not force anyone to follow Him. How do we follow a God who we have not seen? He sent His Son Jesus Christ, as an example of how life should be lived in the earth. God sent his Son Jesus in the world to save us from our sin. The book of Hebrews tells how Jesus lived. He was man that was able to relate to us in every aspect. *"[15]For we don't have a high priest who is unable to empathize with our weaknesses, but we have one who has been tempted in every way, just as we are—yet he did not* sin." Therefore, we are able to "[16] *... approach God's throne of grace with confidence, so that we may receive mercy and find grace to help us in our time of need,"* when we feel that urge to sin. **(Hebrews 4:15-15 AMP)**.

For the believer, the very fact that we sin against God by disobeying His commandments and not allowing Him to conform us to His image demands a change in heart. Paul makes an appeal to us in Romans, *"...in view of [all] the mercies of God, to make a decisive dedication of your bodies [presenting all your members and faculties] as a living sacrifice, holy (devoted, consecrated) and well pleasing to God, which is your reasonable (rational, intelligent) service and spiritual worship."* **(Romans 12:1 AMP)**. Paul also tells us *"Don't be conformed to this world (this age), [fashioned after and adapted to its external, superficial customs], but be transformed (changed) by the [entire] renewal of your mind [by its new ideals and its new attitude], so that you may prove [for yourselves] what is the good and acceptable and perfect will of God, even the thing which is good and acceptable and perfect [in His sight for you]."* **(Romans 12:2 AMP)**.

When sin has infiltrated our hearts, we cannot reflect His image. Everything that prevents us from getting close to God, we must repent. *"If we confess our sins, he is faithful and just and will forgive us our sins and purify us from all unrighteousness."* **(1 John 1:9 NIV)**. John the Baptist tells us in Matthew 3:2 to *"... Repent ([a]think differently; change your mind, regretting your sins and changing your conduct), for the kingdom of heaven is at hand."* **(Matthew 3:2 AMP)**. Everything pertaining to God is at hand. No longer should we live according to our flesh. The world's guidelines distort the human race by accepting certain behaviors and actions that do not glorify God. Sacrifice the things of this world for the Bible tells us "*.... what shall it profit a man, if he shall gain the whole world, and lose his own soul?*" (**Mark 8:36 KJV**). Accepting to follow the image of God through His Son involves repentance; a change in heart. David shares with us in Psalms 66:18, the importance of not regarding iniquity in our hearts *"If I regard iniquity in my heart, the Lord will not hear me."* (**Psalm 66:18 AMP**). According to this scripture, having "regard" for something or someone means that you esteem them highly over another. We do not ever want to regard sin over our Creator God by not changing our actions. Regarding iniquity in one's heart also puts a wall between you and God. The Bible tells us that God cannot look on sin. When a wall is built within an open space, it purpose is to separate one room from another. Just like iniquity, it separates from God. We don't reflect the His image if we are separated from Him through sin.

For the unbeliever, a change involves making a choice in our heart to live for Him. We must forsake our ways and turn to God by asking God to forgive us by not reflecting His image. The Bible tells us that change must first come through accepting Jesus as Lord. *"That if thou shalt confess with thy mouth the Lord Jesus, and shalt believe in thine heart that God hath raised him from the dead, thou shalt be saved. For with the heart man believeth unto righteousness; and with the mouth confession is made unto salvation. For the scripture saith, Whosoever believeth on him shall not be ashamed."*

(Romans 10:9-11 KJV). It involves a change in how we see God and ourselves. Being created in the image of God, we reflect His glory, His holiness, and His mind.

In order to change, I realized it must begin in my heart. Out of the heart come our thoughts, emotions, and actions. Often times, I changed my actions, but not my heart. Many people are sorry for the things that were done because they realized that certain behaviors (sins) did not produce a particular result. When this happens, true repentance does not take place. Repentance takes place when one realizes that the sinful behavior does not reflect God's image. The change requires a turning away from it completely not only in body but in heart. Remember, *"For godly grief and the pain God is permitted to direct, produce a repentance that leads and contributes to salvation and deliverance from evil, and it never brings regret; but worldly grief (the hopeless sorrow that is characteristic of the pagan world) is deadly [breeding and ending in death]."* **(II Corinthians 7:10 AMP).** As we pursue Jesus Christ, Paul tells us to have the mind of Christ, *"Let this same attitude and purpose and [humble] mind be in you which was in Christ Jesus: [Let Him be your example in humility:]"* **(Philippians 2:5 AMP).** Living a life of humility allows us to see God in his fullness. *"For now we are looking in a mirror that gives only a dim (blurred) reflection [of reality asin a riddle or enigma], but then [when perfection comes] we shall see in reality and face to face! Now I know in part (imperfectly), but then I shall know and understandfully and clearly, even in the same manner as I*

have beenfully and clearly known and understood]by God]." **(I Corinthians 13:12 AMP)**. See yourself as God's sees his creation, in His image. Do not allow sin to separate you from the image of your Creator.

<u>PRAYER</u>

Heavenly Father, I thank You and bless Your holy name. I acknowledge You as the Creator God, the giver of all life. I thank You because You have created me in Your image and likeness. According to Your word, You desire to have fellowship with me through Your Son Jesus Christ. According to Your Word in Hebrews Chapter 4, prayer allows us to *"... come boldly unto the throne of grace, that we may obtain mercy, and find grace to help in time of need."* **(Hebrews 4:16 KJV)**. Father, I need You today. Come into my heart and change me so that I may reflect Your image in the earth. No longer do I desire to live according to my flesh, but I want to live according to Your word. It is Your word that changes my actions. Your Word allows me to live out all that You have planned for me. I want a permanent change. I relinquish every part of my will which portrays a false image of You, my Creator and I ask that You will speak Your will in my life. I want to model my life after Your Son Jesus who You sent to die on the cross for my sins. I surrender every part of my life and I ask You to forgive me for dictating my own actions and life. Father, change me so that You will get the glory in my life. In Jesus Name. Amen.

MINISTER FAYE SMITH

Faye Smith, a native of Brandywine, Maryland, serves as an active co-laborer of Timbrel Church International Ministries, under the leadership of Overseer PJ and Executive Chelly Edmund. Presently, she serves as an intercessor and the youth and young adult minister. She is also serves as a member of the Prophetic Intercessors Council of an Empowered People (PICEP) where she is an intense prophetic intercessor ministering the heart and purposes of God.

Minister Faye's sincere desire is for the "hurting" to be healed and to teach young women how to walk in the fullness of God. Moreover, she continues to lend her prayers and words of encouragement in helping others reach their full potential in Christ. A woman in pursuit of the Kingdom of God, Minister Faye's vision and goals are to empower and equip believers for Kingdom living and it is expressed through the ministries of teaching and intercession.

CHAPTER 7

A Supernatural Transformation

In August 1988, I experienced what seemed to be one of the darkest moments of my life. I had emotionally hit rock bottom. It was at that time I realized my marriage was over and it felt like my life was over as well. I was only 25 years old and a mother of a two-year-old son.

As I sat alone in my living room a series of questions were going through my mind. What was I going to do? Should I stay or leave? Where would I go? Could I take care of my son and myself? How would I make it without my husband? I loved this man more than life itself. He was my best friend, my knight in shining armor, my hero, and my savior.

You see my husband had rescued me from a life that had caused me much pain, but now I was experiencing an even greater pain. This pain was unbearable, because it felt like my heart had been torn into a million pieces never to be put back together again. I was deeply depressed and lost. I just did not know what to do. This problem was so much bigger than I was. Who could fix it? Who was able to fix me?

Suddenly, I remembered this man named Jesus that had been talked so much about in the church. I didn't go to church on a regular basis nor did I have a personal relationship with Jesus Christ. I knew of Him, but I really didn't know Him. It was at that moment that I realized I needed this man named Jesus in my life. I had tried everything and everybody hoping that they could fill the void and remove the pain that was so deep within my heart. I then fell on my knees with tears rolling down my face saying, "Lord Jesus, help me please. If you are real, please come into my life."

After speaking those words, the glory and the presence of the Lord filled the room. I felt His glory, His presence, His power, His peace, His joy, His forgiveness, but most of all I felt His unconditional love for me. I had never experienced a love like that before.

While I was having this supernatural encounter with Jesus, something supernaturally was taking place on the inside of me. I really didn't understand exactly what was happening, but I knew I was different in some way. I had become a believer of Jesus Christ, because He had made Himself so real to me. I am a firm believer that if you ever have a true encounter with our Lord and Savior Jesus Christ you can never remain the same.

The next day it was very evident to others that something had happened to me. They said, "What has happened to you? You look different. You seem different. You have changed. You are not cursing and using bad language anymore." I then told them about my encounter with Jesus and how I had become born again. You see before my encounter with Jesus I used bad language and cursed constantly. Every other word that came out of my mouth was a curse word, but through that one encounter with Jesus, I had been instantly delivered from that particular behavior. It was at that moment I realized that I was being transformed by the power and glory of God.

Some of you may be saying to yourselves, "What about the marriage? Did Jesus fix it?" My response to you would be, "No. He didn't fix the marriage, but He started the process of fixing me." You see fixing me was His top priority at that time, because I was lost and on my way to hell. Jesus loved me so much that He did not want me to go to hell, but He wanted me to have eternal life. Not only that, but He had other plans for my life. *"For I know the plans I have for you," declares the Lord, "plans to prosper you and not to harm you, plans to give you hope and a future."* **(Jeremiah 29:11 NIV).**

Even though my marriage ended, many incredible miracles and blessings came out of that dark season of my life. First, I became a born again believer of Jesus Christ, and I was sold out for Him. I found myself being so in love with Him. He was now my husband, my best friend, my knight in shining armor, my hero, and my SAVIOR and LORD. Secondly, God had blessed me with a son, and I was so thankful for such a precious gift. Thirdly, my son and I had everything we needed, and we never went lacking for anything. I could see God's hand at work so strongly in my life, and I was very grateful unto Him for it.

Now, that I was a born again believer, my son and I were always present in the house of the Lord. I was so broken and emotionally messed up from so many things that had happened to me in my life. I needed Jesus to heal me everywhere I hurt. I needed to be delivered and set free from many things. I knew if Jesus did it before (instantly being delivered from cursing and using bad language) He could do it again. After all, He was the one who had started this transformation on the inside of me.

I also wanted to obtain a solid biblical foundation in Jesus Christ and to learn as much as I could about the Kingdom of God. I wanted to know more about Him. Through hearing the preaching and teaching of God's word, I found myself growing in leaps and bounds. I was soaking it all up like a sponge, and my heart was wide open for the things of God.

I then began experiencing His presence and having supernatural encounters with Him more and more. The more I received of Him the hungrier I became for Him. I was constantly being transformed by His power and glory repeatedly. My life had drastically changed for the better, and I had become a completely different person. I found myself being healed, delivered, and made free from many things. Even the void and pain I once had in my heart was now gone, and I was completely whole in Christ Jesus.

I also had a better understanding of why Jesus responded so strongly to me in my living room that day and why He was still responding to me. It was not because I was praying these awesome prayers, because I did not know anything about prayer at that time. The reason Jesus was responding was because He was sensing a heart of worship and true repentance. You see a heart of worship and true repentance will draw Jesus close to you. If you become intimate with Him, He will become intimate with you.

You may be saying to yourself, "What is a heart of true repentance?" When someone has a heart of true repentance, they are acknowledging to themselves and to God that they have committed some type of sin whether it is through past behaviors or actions, misdeeds, moral shortcomings, etc. This person will experience a deep conviction of regret and remorse for what they have done. They feel such sympathy that they will make a confession and apology to God or to man (if necessary) asking them for their forgiveness. They will even go as far as making a decision and commitment to turn away from that particular sin to make a change for the better in their lives. I believe as Christians we sometimes forget that the concept of true repentance is not only used at the time of salvation, but it should be used whenever sin is present in our lives.

You see I was deeply sorry for my wrong thinking and my wrong doings. Most of my young adult life I had sinned against God in many ways. The thing that bothered me most was how I had been searching for love in all the wrong places. I was trying to fill the void and remove the pain that was deep within my heart when Jesus was there all the time wanting to love on me. He was always trying to get my attention, but I did not know it was Him at that time. I didn't realize Jesus was speaking to me until after I had been taught the word of God.

I was receiving dreams from the Lord at a young age, and I was hearing His voice very clearly as a teenager. His calm and still voice brought me much peace in the midst of confusion. There were many times I saw adults doing certain things, and I would hear the voice of the Lord speaking to me concerning those situations. At that time, He was teaching me what was right, what was wrong, what to do, and what not to do. He was even trying to lead me in the right direction concerning my own life as well. There were times I listened to His voice, but there were many times I did not listen and there were consequences for my disobedience. I realized I needed God's forgiveness, grace, and mercy towards me. The key to receiving those things from Him was through a heart of worship and true repentance. A heart of worship and true repentance brings forth a great transformation in our lives.

You may be saying to yourself, "You don't know what I've done. Jesus will never forgive me." No, I don't know what you've done, but I do know what the word of God has to say about it. *"If we confess our sins, he is faithful and just to forgive us our sins, and to cleanse us from all unrighteousness."* **(I John 1:9 KJV).** *"For I will be merciful to their unrighteousness, and their sins and their iniquities will I remember no more."* **(Hebrews 8:12 KJV).** *"That if thou shalt confess with thy mouth the Lord Jesus, and shalt believe in thine heart that God hath raised him from the dead, thou shalt be saved."* **(Romans 10:9 KJV).** Has Jesus been trying to get your attention? Has He been knocking on the door of your heart? If so, I pray on today that you will open the door and allow Him to come in. Once you accept Him and allow Him to come in, you too will be transformed by the power and glory of God.

It is hard to believe that over 24 years ago I received Jesus Christ as my personal Savior. I can honestly say that it was the best decision I ever made in my life. I cannot even imagine my life now without Him. He has proven Himself faithful to me over and over again. I have to say that I have learned a lot over these past 24 years walking with the Lord. It has been through my life experiences that I have been able to help others in their lives.

One of the things I've learned is that Jesus has the power to change any situation that we may be facing. Sometimes He will allow a situation to make a change in us to accomplish His perfect will in our lives. Even though the process can be very painful and difficult at times, we need to embrace whatever He is doing in our lives. He truly knows what is best for us. As believers of Jesus Christ it is important that we trust Him completely even when we do not understand. *"⁵Trust in the Lord with all thine heart; and lean not unto thine own understanding. ⁶In all thy ways acknowledge him, and he shall direct thy paths."* **(Proverbs 3:5-6 KJV)**. *"For as the heavens are higher than the earth, so are my ways higher than your ways, and my thoughts than your thoughts."* **(Isaiah 55:9 KJV)**.

I would like to leave you with this little nugget of wisdom. If you are ever faced with going through the process of allowing a situation to change you, I ask you to please guard your heart during that time. If you don't guard your heart, you will find yourself becoming frustrated, angry, resentful, and even bitter towards God for not changing your situation. Never allow these negative emotions to take root in your heart, because they will only separate you from the Lord. As soon as you start experiencing these emotions, immediately uproot them through prayer with a heart of worship and true repentance.

CLOSING PRAYER

Heavenly Father,

I truly thank You for giving me this opportunity to share just a portion of my testimony with my brother or my sister. May it encourage them and give them hope. I do not know what they may be facing or going through at this very moment, but I do know that YOU are the only one who can fill the void and remove the pain deep within their heart. YOU are the only one who can heal them everywhere they hurt. YOU are the only one who can deliver them and make them free. I pray right now that they would seek You and have a heart of worship and true repentance, which will bring forth a great transformation in their lives. Lord Jesus, I ask You now to allow them to have a supernatural encounter with You where they will experience Your glory, Your presence, Your power, Your peace, Your joy, Your forgiveness, but most of all Your unconditional love towards them. Let them know that this is not the season to give up and die, but this is the season to live.

So, right now, I declare and decree, in the name of Jesus, that you will not give up and die in this season but you will live and declare the works of the Lord. I declare and decree, in the name of Jesus, that God will give you beauty for your ashes. And what the devil meant for evil God will turn it all around for your good. I declare and decree, in the name of Jesus, that you will fulfill every God ordained assignment that God has assigned for your hands to do. You will fulfill the calling that is upon your life, and you will reach your destiny. I declare and decree, in the name of Jesus, that you will be an ambassador and a change agent in the earth making a difference for our Lord and Savior Jesus Christ. I pray all these things now and seal them with the blood of Jesus. In Jesus precious name, Amen.

MINISTER LINDA MOODY

Minister Linda Moody loves preaching and teaching the word of God as well as ministering to those who are hurting. Her greatest joy in ministry is seeing lives transformed by the power and glory of God.

In 1997, Minister Moody was licensed to preach the Gospel of Jesus Christ. She has been actively involved in the local church for approximately 20 years and has held positions such as: Teacher, Workshop Instructor, Youth Pastor, Counselor, Mentor for youth and young adults, and has served on the Altar Response Ministry and Corporate Prayer Team Ministry.

Minister Moody is also known for spear heading powerful and life changing workshops for the body of Christ, which are taught under the anointing and power of God. These workshops include: Marriage Boot C. A. M. P. (Counseling and Marriage Preparation); and Sexually Transmitted Diseases (STDs) Awareness Workshops. Through these workshops, many lives have been changed.

She is a Professional Clinical Member of the National Christian Counselors Association where she is certified as a Temperament Counselor and a licensed Clinical Pastoral Counselor. She has an Associate Degree in Biblical Studies, Bachelor Degree in Theology, and Masters Degree in Clinical Christian Counseling.

Minister Moody has ministered in Virginia, Maryland, Washington DC, and Delaware. She has also traveled to the Nation of Africa where her life was changed forever. She was privileged to minister in South Africa, Botswana, and Zambia.

VOLUME IV - RIGHTEOUSNESS

TABLE OF CONTENTS

VOLUME IV RIGHTEOUSNESS

CHAPTER 1

The Fruit of Righteousness

"²²But the fruit of the [Holy] Spirit [the work which His presence within accomplishes] is love, joy (gladness), peace, patience (an even temper, forbearance), kindness, goodness (benevolence), faithfulness, Gentleness (meekness, humility), self-control (self-restraint, continence). ²³Against such things there is no law [that can bring a charge]." **(Galatians 5:22-23 AMP)**

There have been many transitions in my life over the past few years. God has seen me through some of the toughest times and greatest times. Prayer, fasting, faith and favor undergirded the ups and downs of life. There is no explanation for the evidence of endurance displayed during this season except for the grace of God. The sudden death of my mother from brain cancer, followed by the death of the patriarch of my family and then the death of my aunt was the beginning of a tough time for my family. A year later my sister was diagnosed with terminal lung cancer and my daughter-in-law passed away without cause at the age of thirty-three. All of these circumstances tested my faith and righteousness. I wanted to cave in, give up and throw in the towel all at the same time. Like most people, there is a limit to what I thought I could bear. I am a witness that God knows no limits. He is the sustainer of our souls in the midst of tribulation. Our righteousness does not eliminate our suffering. In fact the Bible declares *"Many are the afflictions of the righteous, But the Lord delivers him out of them all."* **(Psalm 34:19 NKJV).** We all have to learn to be like Job and wait until our change comes.

In these times of swift transition, I have found solace in the consistency of Jesus in my life. His presence is comforting and compelling. The presence of the Lord has helped maintain my faith and the inspiration of the Holy Spirit has kept me motivated beyond my life experiences. The truth is our life experiences whether good or bad shape our interpretation of the role of God in our lives and our access to God through our prayer life. When things are going well and according to our plan, we feel in some ways closer to God. When life is filled with disappointments, discouragement and despair, we take on the worldview of King David. *"How long, Lord? Will you forget me forever? How long will you hide your face from me?* ¹ *How long must I wrestle with my thoughts and day after day have sorrow in my heart? How long will my enemy triumph over me?* ²*"* **(Psalm 13:1-2 NIV).** These questions have run through my mind many times when I was under attack from the enemy, hurt from friendly fire or by my own self-inflicted wounds. Whatever the case may be, it hurts to suffer. The fruit of our suffering is a mature walk with God. This is witnessed by our steadfastness in serving, sacrificing and submitting even when it would be easier to give up. We are reminded by the Apostle Peter of this very predicament.

"Beloved, don't be amazed and bewildered at the fiery ordeal which is taking place to test your quality, as though something strange were befalling you" (I Peter 4:12 AMP). All of life's unexpected twists and turns may take us by surprise but they are no surprise to God. In fact, these are the instruments that God uses to prove the authenticity of our faith.

Many times as Christians, we take our level of faith and the sanctification process for granted. We believe that with time both our faith and sanctity will increase without much effort on our part. Growing in righteousness is a lifelong process that can only be achieved through a genuine relationship with Jesus Christ. The Holy Spirit brings about this transformation by activating our inborn character traits instilled in every Christian upon salvation. These magnificent transformers are the same character traits that Jesus modeled and expects us to exhibit in the life of holiness we are called to live. What an awesome Savior. He provides us with the tools necessary for right living.

The tools, traits and characteristics I am describing are none other than the fruit of the Spirit.

Galatians 5 spells out the ingredients for righteous living in these nine succinct descriptions of life in the Spirit: love, joy, peace, patience, kindness, goodness, faithfulness, gentleness and self-control. They are listed not in order of importance, but notably with love at the beginning, and self-control at the end. You need both of these to get through the ones in the middle. The definition given for fruit of the Spirit in the book, *The Fruit of the Spirit: Cultivating Christian Character* by Stuart Briscoe states, "The fruit of the Spirit is to be seen not as a collection of unrelated fruits that can be selected or neglected according to personal preference, but rather as a composite description of all-around behavior that is the direct result of a relationship with the living Lord who indwells his people by his Spirit"[15]. In other words, you cannot pick and choose which fruit you will have. As a believer, we must exhibit all of the fruit as the representation of our character in Christ. It is more important to be godly than gifted. We can develop our faith and our fruit when we cover ourselves in prayer.

Love is the cornerstone of our faith in Christ. It is no accident that it is also the first fruit of the Spirit and one of the gifts the Holy Spirit has given us. Without love, the remaining fruit cannot be as effective. Love is not to be dispersed conditionally, but without reservation. **Romans 13:8** challenge us to *"owe no man anything, except to love one another"* **(AMP)**. This is sometimes easier said than done. Living a life of love is a commandment given to us by Jesus. It is in us but bearing the fruit of love is not so easy. The Apostle Paul gives us the definition of agape love in **I Corinthians 13**. Ultimately, we are responsible to love one another because God has first loved us. In the end, love never fails and will prevail when all other alternatives have been exhausted.

The second fruit of the Spirit is joy. Our joy is attacked more than any of the others because it is the source of our strength. In the book of Nehemiah, the prophet encouraged the Israelites to celebrate the words of the law and do not be sad at its requirements but to rejoice in the Lord. The Philippians were encouraged to "rejoice in the Lord always". This does not mean we will always have joyful moments but that the Lord gives us joy. He is the source of our joy so it is something we have access to 24/7. It is not something we have to search for. We can love and be joyful because of the sacrifice Jesus made out of love and obedience to God.

Peace is the ability to live out the serenity prayer as a lifestyle. The peace of God should not be overlooked as an attribute of Christians. When chaos breaks out all around us, we should be at peace within and with whatever life brings our way. Accepting those things we cannot change does not mean giving up; it is acknowledging the situation and then choosing to respond with peace. This is difficult for some of us to internalize. In our society, we like to fix situations, people and determine outcomes. God's "peace that surpasses understanding" helps us to be content in every circumstance. We become more than conquerors when we submit our will to God and accept His will. Patience and peace are like fraternal twins. They have some of the same characteristics but also are different enough to be distinct. Patience requires humility and trust. *As you know, we count as blessed those who have persevered. You have heard of Job's perseverance and have seen what the Lord finally brought about."* **(James 5:11 NIV).** Waiting is one of the disciplines that must be learned and it only comes through experience. Waiting with a heart of expectancy is the best option for manifesting patience. Being patient helps keep us from becoming weary in our kingdom work and allows us to cultivate an attitude of kindness and goodness.

Kindness and goodness are our outward actions towards others. These are the fruit of the Spirit that people can readily identify as attributes of Christians. Kindness is having compassion towards people and showing them that you care about them. It is love in action. We can be kind and thoughtful toward others in spite of their mistreatment of us. Our kindness spills over into goodness, which is treating others with decency and integrity. It is the tangible aspect of our fruit. Goodness is displayed in our treatment of others in the area of giving and serving. It is not an inward action but an outward expression of our faith. In layman terms, goodness answers the question, 'What have you done for me lately?' How has your fruit affected the life of another? Honestly answering these questions could give you a reality check in your acts of the faith.

Faithfulness and gentleness represent our commitment and humility in our Christian walk. In Hebrews 11, a record of the people of God who were models of faith has been listed. Their faith counted as righteousness because they stuck with the assignment God gave them no matter the personal cost. The psalmist declared, *"I have chosen the way of truth and faithfulness; Your ordinances have I set before me."* **(Psalm 119:30 AMP)**. Faithfulness has to be a conscious commitment made because of our love for God. It is not something that comes naturally to us for we would betray ourselves if exposed to the right temptation. Humility and meekness comprise gentleness. Our natural inclination is to be prideful and self-sufficient. We do not want to show any neediness or weakness because of this we sometimes are not gentle in our dealings with others. We sometimes are forced into humility like King David who prayed this in **Psalm 51** after being confronted by Nathan the prophet. *"Create in me a clean heart, O God, and renew a right, persevering, and steadfast spirit within me."* **(Psalm 51:10 KJV)**. Gentleness is evident after we give our will to God.

The final and most challenging fruit is self-control. Taming the wild beast of selfishness and entitlement that is prevalent in our churches is one of the most challenging for leaders to manage. Each of us has our own agenda and submitting our will to the Holy Spirit is what we need the most. When you use restraint and modesty when making choices, this is the fruit of self-control. Learning to tell yourself 'no' is the best solution to our anything goes frame of mind. The Apostle Paul reminds us that *"All things are lawful for me, but all things are not helpful ... I will not be brought under the power of any."* **(I Corinthians 6:12 NKJV).** We have the freedom to choose as a benefit of grace and mercy. We are to use our freedom for good and not for evil; for the kingdom and not for ourselves. Self-control is having discipline when it is a challenge. This fruit of the Spirit can save us from a lot of grief. It is often dismissed, but can become our best tool as we strive to be like Christ.

It is not only the presence of the Fruit of the Spirit that gives evidence of spiritual growth and righteousness. It is the manifestation of the behaviors that signify the motives of our hearts. It is not what is on the outside of a person that makes them holy. It is what comes out of them that give witness to their faith and more importantly of their God. Jesus said His food was to do the will of the Father. Everything Jesus did was out of a desire to please God. When righteousness is a priority in our lives, those around us will witness the fruit of the Spirit in action. James reminds us that faith without works is dead. How will we be known as people of prayer and purpose with nothing to show for it? Not that we have to prove ourselves to the world but we are the only Bible some people will ever read. We are the Body of Christ. We must represent Jesus and ensure that our fruit genuinely represents Him.

PRAYER

Lord even though our righteousness is like filthy rags You allow us to come boldly to Your throne of grace. We have not always sought to please You but our prayer is that we have a heart like Yours. We desire a heart of love and compassion so that we can receive what we pray for. Give us a clean heart and a humble spirit that is obedient to Your will. This prayer is not for selfish ambition but so You will get the glory out of our life. In pursuit of fame and fortune, we have forgotten the most precious blessing of all Your grace and mercy. As we seek to look like You, act like You and obey Your will, help us to produce fruit that will last. We need to be real with You and confess our faults so that we can receive the good things You have in store for us. We love you. Amen.

MINISTER CARLA J. DEBNAM

Minister Carla J. Debnam MS, LCPC is the wife of Bishop Dwayne C. Debnam and an associate minister of Morning Star Baptist Church, Catonsville, MD. She has a Master of Science degree in Pastoral Counseling from Loyola University Maryland and is currently pursuing a Doctor of Ministry degree in Transformational Leadership from the Ashland Theological Seminary in Ashland, Ohio. Minister Debnam is a Licensed Clinical Professional Counselor (LCPC) in Maryland. She is a member of the American Counseling Association, the American Association of Christian Counselors and Delta Sigma Theta Sorority, Inc. where she serves as chaplain of the Columbia (MD) Alumnae chapter. She has written articles on mental health topics and frequently presents at workshops and conferences.

Minister Debnam has a passion for people and often ministers in the prisons and nursing homes. In 2006, Minister Debnam along with two other pastor's wives founded the Leading Ladies Ministry, a fellowship of support and renewal for pastor's wives.

She is the mother of Corey, Jewell and Jared and grandmother of Courtney.   She enjoys spending time with her family, reading and baking and stands on the promise of Philippians 1:6, *"Being confident of this, that he who began a good work in you will carry it on to completion until the day of Christ Jesus."* (**NIV**)

CHAPTER 2

Never Give Up

The purpose for writing this chapter serves as an opportunity to offer up encouragement to the saved, the unsaved and to those who may have or might be experiencing a period of loneliness in their life. When it seems as though God was silent, but you still yearn to hear from Him because when you are faced with the issues and the hurts of life, you know where your help comes from.

I believe that we are truly living in a world where there is a great cloud of disappointment, rejection and pain. We often find that life is not what we want it to be or what it should be and we even feel that life is not fair. There are those who are down in the dumps or in the depths of life circumstances, which most often leads them to feeling that there is no reason to keep on living. They constantly struggle with issues, problems and the conflicts of life. They find themselves feeling guilty about the struggles to which they have attributed. We must remember that the God we serve is a God of a second chance and all we have to do is to ask for forgiveness for everything that we do that is not according to the word of God.

"¹Wherefore seeing we also are compassed about with so great a cloud of witness, let us lay aside every weight, and the sin which doth so easily beset us and let us run with patience

the race that is set before us. ²Looking unto Jesus the author and finisher of our faith; who for the joy that was set before him endured the cross, despising the shame and is set down at the right hand of the throne of God." **(Hebrews 12:1-2 KJV).**

Here, we have the illustration of an athlete that is running a marathon and who has prepared for the race. Jesus provides the ultimate model of endurance for us to keep pressing although we face unplanned sufferings, hurt and other uncertainties that we may be going through. Jesus endured the agony of the cross. He knew what He had to go through for you and me. Although He knew He would face indescribable distress, He knew that there would be joy after the pain and He would be at His Father's right hand in heaven. Giving up should never be an option for any of us but it is a choice that we choose to make.

It is how we look at the circumstances and the situations in our life that determines the outcome of how we face the victory or the defeat in life. Our victory comes through our faith and belief in Jesus Christ. We have to learn that the ways we think about things are not what God has planned for you and me. I had to experience and am learning that this Christian walk encompasses hard work. We will have to give up the things that could come between God and us. God is a jealous God and nothing comes before Him. I believe that the despair, difficulties and disappointments that we experience is nothing more than training and preparation to help us increase our spiritual maturity in God.

"¹If ye then be risen with Christ seek those things which are above, where Christ sitteth on the right hand of God. ²Set your affection on things above, not on things on the earth. ³

For ye are dead, and your life is hid with Christ in God. ³"
(Colossians 3:1-3 KJV).

In what we deem as failures or setbacks, rather than seeking approval from the world, we must look to Christ and live for what God has predetermined for your life. After experiencing interferences, being condemned and even talked about, we ought to learn to be like the Apostle Paul. He reminds us"…**my strength is made perfect in weakness**" **(II Corinthians 12:9 KJV).** We must come to realize that whatever the deficiency we think we have, we must know that God knew what they were before we did. Paul asked the Lord three times to remove his thorn but God would not because the thorn served as a purpose in Paul's life. We all have something in our lives we want God to remove, but it is there to get to us to a place where we must trust Him in all things.

God allows us to go through things in our lives so that He can accomplish what He has already mapped out for our lives. Our imperfections, our looks, how we think or even speak does not matter. In other words, difficult times for us are an indication that God is molding and shaping us to become more like Him.

"⁹And he said unto me, My grace is sufficient for thee: for my strength is made perfect in weakness. Most gladly therefore will I rather glory in my infirmities that the power of Christ may rest upon me. ¹⁰Therefore I take pleasure in infirmities in reproaches, in necessities in persecutions, in distresses for Christ's sake: for when I am weak, then am I strong." **(II Corinthians 12:9-10 KJV).**

God created you and me because He knew what we would go through in life. It is in our weakness and our feeling of hopelessness that we find our strength in God. God is able to use us in ways we could never even imagine. We must be like the Christians at the Church of Colossian when Paul told them that in order to experience joy they first must learn how to endure and respond to the trials and tribulations with an eternal perspective. Paul reminds them that they are not alone. God is with them every step of the way. We were created in God's imagine and the ups and downs we go through is part of His plan. In this life, we must realize that God knows each one of us and knows our beginning and our end. We are His most precious creation and He wants us to have a relationship with Him.

"¹O Lord thou hast searched me and known me. ²Thou knowest my downsitting and mine uprising, thou understandest my though afar off. ³Thou compassest my path and my lying down and art acquainted with all my ways." **(Psalms 139:1-3 KJV).**

My brothers and sisters we will have trials and temptations. We cannot give up when things are not so pretty. I am here to tell you, hang in there because God will not put more on you than you can bear.

We live in a broken world. <u>Yes, it seems as though bad things happen to good people.</u> Believers also face times of anxiety, despair and darkness. Know, that there is nothing that seems to be unusual or unspiritual about you. I feel down from time to time. You are not alone. You may be up one moment and down the next day.

"¹Therefore being justified by faith, we have peace with God through our Lord Jesus Christ. ²By whom also we have access by faith into this grace, wherein we stand, and rejoice in hope of the glory of God. ³And not only so, but we glory

in tribulations also; knowing that tribulation worketh patience; ⁴and patience, experience and experience, hope. ⁵And hope maketh not ashamed, because the love of God is shed abroad in our hearts by the Holy Ghost which is given unto us." (Romans 5:1-5 KJV).

What do you do when the enemy wants you to feel and believe that perhaps God has forgotten you or He just does not care? As I prayed about this assignment, I struggled with having to write this. I experienced a period in my life when the more I prayed the more things seem to get worse. However, I continued to pray to God. I am reminded of Peter in his teaching to the Christians that regardless of their circumstances, rejoice. It is not knowledge alone but the Word of God and their faith that causes the believer to experience joy and fearlessness even in the face of persecution and suffering. My brothers and sisters, God does answer prayers. What I experienced in my life took me to another level of maturity in God. I know without a shadow of doubt that there is hope when you believe in the word of God. I learned that when I am persecuted, it is an opportunity to be an example and love those who persecute you. I learned that I am not in control. God is in control.

"¹I waited patiently for the Lord and he inclined unto me and heard my cry. ²He brought me up also out of a horrible pit, out of the miry clay, and set my feet upon a rock and established my goings. ³And he hath put a new song in my mouth, even praise unto our God: many shall see it, and fear and shall trust in the Lord." (Psalm 40:1-3 KJV).

No matter how bad it may seem just, know that God has a solution to every problem that may be facing today. Remember that our present trials, no matter how hard they may seem are nothing compared to eternal fire for those who reject Jesus. I learned how to wait on God. When you wait on God He will turn your hurt and pain into joy. Do not give up on God because He will not give up on you.

"⁸We are troubled on every side, yet not distressed: we are perplexed, but not in despair; ⁹Persecuted, but not forsaken; cast down, but not destroyed." **(II Corinthians 4:8-9 KJV).**

The Apostle Paul was trying to get the Corinthian church to see the grace of God at work in his life. Paul trials were so overwhelming and he was hard pressed on every side, perplexed, persecuted and struck down. Yet, he never gave up. Instead, he encouraged the people not to lose heart in hard times but to continue to trust God. The lesson for you and me is that if Paul had the determination to continue regardless of what it looked like then why can't you and I strive and believe God for what he can and will do for us. We have to believe what God promised in His word that He would never leave us or forsake us. He will be with us always. We must endure the hardships and believe that God will take care of our every need. He will see us through.

"Be strong and of a good courage, fear not, nor be afraid of them for the Lord thy God, he it is that doth go with thee; he will not fail thee, nor forsake thee." **(Deuteronomy 31:6 KJV).**

I made a decision to serve and live for Christ and to strive for His righteousness because God loves us so much that He gave His only begotten son to die for the sins of this world.

"¹³Brethren, I count not myself to have apprehended: but

*this one thing I do, forgetting those things which are behind and reaching forth unto those things which are before. *[14]*I press toward the mark for the prize of the high calling of God in Christ Jesus."* (Philippians 3:13-14 KJV).

My brothers and sisters the equation is simple in order to know Jesus Christ as your Lord and Savior.

"[6]*But the righteousness which is of faith speaketh on this wise, Say not in thine heart, Who shall ascend into Heaven (that is to bring Christ down from above). *[7]*Or, Who shall descend into the deep (that is, to bring up Christ again from the dead). *[8]*But what saith it? The word is nigh thee even in thy mouth and in thy heart: that is the word of faith which we preach; *[9]*That if thou shalt confess with thy mouth the Lord Jesus and shalt believe in thine heart that God hath raised him from the dead thou shalt be saved."* (Romans 10:6-9 KJV).

As I close this chapter, I would like to leave this with you. Never give up because our sufferings are a reminder that if we continue, we have an eternal future.

"[17]*The righteous cry, and the Lord heareth, and delivereth them out of all their troubles. *[18]*The Lord is nigh unto them that are of a broken heart and saveth such as be of a contrite spirit. *[19]*Many are the afflictions of the righteous: but the Lord delivereth him out of them all."* (Psalm 34:17-19 KJV).

Pray with me: Thank you God for allowing me for this time and purpose to share with others how awesome You are that it not over until You say it is over. I thank You for your grace and mercy in directing me in this project so that somebody may be saved or rededicate their life to You. You continue to provide for us in spite of all our shortcomings. God thank You for Your promise that You will give us what is needed to get through the good and the bad. Lord, thank You for the many times you delivered me in the past and thank You in advance for the many times you will deliver me in the future. Finally, God, thank You for sustaining us through the sufferings that we face and to know that You are always with us. Lord, help us to humble ourselves and learn to turn to You in times of trouble. Amen.

ELDER GREGORY A. ARMSTRONG

Elder Gregory A. Armstrong, the son of Theodore A. Armstrong and Missionary Eunice Cobb, is a native of Kingsland, Georgia and was educated in the Camden County school system. He attended Savannah State College in Savannah Georgia where he studied accounting. He graduated with a Bachelor of Science degree in Accounting in June of 1982.

Elder Armstrong received his early spiritual growth and nurturing at the Church of Victory Tabernacle, Atlanta, Georgia, under the leadership of Bishop Carolyn Horton. He has served faithfully to his church for over 15 years under the leadership of the late Elder Herbert B. Chambers, Pastor James Johnson and his current Pastor Gloria Eiland.

Understanding the need to study to show thyself approved, Elder Armstrong is a Graduate of the Trinity College of the Bible and Theological Seminary with a Master of Arts in Pastoral Ministry, in preparation for the call to ministry. He is a lay-counselor where he works in the field of marriage, grief, youth, young adults, and men.

Elder Armstrong currently serves as the Assistant Pastor of Young's Memorial Church of Christ Holiness, UHCA Washington, D.C. He serves as the Pastor of Men's Ministry, Sunday School Superintendent, and Trustee Board, Pastor of Couple's Ministry and the Pastor over the Music Ministry. Elder Armstrong was ordained as an elder by the Board of Presbyterian of the United Holy Church of America on June 11, 2005.

Elder Armstrong is happily married to Minister Betty Armstrong. He sincerely believes that without her love, support and encouragement, many of his goals would not have been accomplished. He is the father of one beautiful daughter, Shamira.

CHAPTER 3

Living Free From Your Past

How is your love life? Love is the foundation for everything that we receive from Father God. In experiencing that love, it brings a confidence, a comfort in knowing that God loves me, God accepts me, God invites me into His presence, and God wants a relationship with me.

When you are intimately connected to the love of God, you will come to know your position in the kingdom of God. That place or position is called "right standing with God or Righteousness." Righteousness is a position, a place in God where you have no hesitation, no reserve when you approach him. "Jesus was made so Righteous that He could enter into the presence of the Father with no sense of sin or guilt or inferiority."[16] We have been given the "right" to enter as he did. We are joint-heirs with Jesus Christ, which makes us, welcome to come before the Father because the blood of Jesus cleansed us, and made us right with the Father.

Do you realize that you are made right with God? "[22] **We are made right with God by placing our faith in Jesus Christ. And this is true for everyone who believes, no matter who we are. [23] For everyone has sinned; we all fall short of God's glorious** standard. ²⁴ *Yet God, with undeserved kindness, declares that we are righteous. He did this through Christ Jesus when he freed us from the penalty for our sins.* ²⁵ *For God presented Jesus as the sacrifice for sin. People are made right with God when they believe that Jesus sacrificed his life, shedding his blood. This sacrifice shows that God was being fair when he held back and did not punish those who sinned in times past,* ²⁶ *for he was looking ahead and including them in what he would do in this present time. God did this to demonstrate his righteousness, for he himself is fair and just, and he declares sinners to be right in his sight when they believe in Jesus."* **(Romans 3:22-26 New Living Translation NLT).** So, now through faith in Christ, we are made right with God **(Galatians 3:24)**.

First, you must believe that you are righteous before you can live righteous. Believe and accept that the work of Jesus on the cross was powerful enough to satisfy the penalty for sin and that your sins were wiped clean. Therefore, you have no past. **Colossians 2:14 (AMP)…** *the debt was cancelled and wiped away.* That means there is no record of your past sins, no matter how ugly, terrible, despicable, or disgusting they were. God said it was wiped clean, blotted out (no trace). In other words, there is no evidence of your past sins as far as God is concerned.

When I was born again, one of the first things that was so precious to me that I grabbed hold of was healing. The second was that my past sins were forgiven. That was the beginning of my deliverance from the old sin nature. To know that my past life was now behind me was a weight lifted; a freedom that is not matched by anything. As I learned that, I had to admit my sin to myself and then to God, not to any priest or minister, the process of repenting began. I was then able to, by faith shake off the past hurts and disappointments. We all had to admit at one point that we were sinners and had to repent, in order to be born again.

Repent[17] is defined in Vine's Dictionary as "to change one's mind or purpose, involving both a turning from sin and a turning to God." This is where you make that heart decision that you are done with that sin and you're not doing it again, and really mean it. The act of repentance is absolutely necessary to stay free. We have all made mistakes and said or done things we wished we could take back. I have learned that in order to stay free from guilt or condemnation I have to repent, not hanging on to anything. Thankfully, as I conform to Christ's image, I don't have to repent as often as I used to for that slip of the tongue or that bad decision I made. The more I know God; His word changes my heart, my attitude, and my relationship with Christ. I am no longer having pity parties, and beating myself up mentally for days or weeks is not part of my life anymore. That proved wasteful and a hindrance to my prayer life.

When I realize I have not been kind, spoke harshly, or did not walk in love, I have trained myself with the help of the Holy Spirit to repent quickly and as we now say, "to keep it moving." God knows exactly what we did, when we did it, and why we did it. Guess what, He is not shocked. No, He wants us to follow His plan and repent, receive forgiveness, forget it and move on which is not a long drawn out process.

Far too many people are living outside of salvation because of condemnation. Many have not dared to come to church because of feeling unworthy. In their minds, they have lived such a terrible life; they have messed up so bad that there is no way that God would accept them. They are living a life of shame and wake up not expecting anything good to happen to them because of their past. If we ourselves are free from guilt and shame, we can share this with others, Christians and non- Christians. God wants us to live that way now that we are in His family and a part of the kingdom of heaven. God is a good God and He wants us to share with anybody and everybody that He is willing to forgive them of their past. *"For God made Christ, who never sinned, to be the offering for our sin,[a] so that we could be made right with God through Christ."* **(II Corinthians 5:21 NLT).**

Consider Paul, how could he be so bold and say*"Trust us. We've never hurt a soul, never exploited or taken advantage of anyone?"* **(II Corinthians 7:2 Message).** This is the man who was consenting of Stephen's stoning death and much persecution of the church (see Acts 8:1-3; 9:1). Yet he was unashamed to say he had wronged no man, hurt no man. He got the revelation that he was forgiven of his past and he accepted his righteousness. Paul says *"Brethren , I count not myself to have apprehended, but this one thing I do, forgetting those things which are behind , and reaching forward to those things which are ahead."* **(Philippians 3:13 NKJV).**

When you were born-again and received Jesus Christ as your Lord and Savior you became a new creature. *"Anyone united with the Messiah gets a fresh start, is created new. The old life is gone."* (**2 Corinthians 5:17 Message)**. Praise God, Your life is ahead, not behind you. Our place now is to move forward. If it was good, praise God for the good, if it was not so good, repent, confess it and RECEIVE the forgiveness God has already provided for you in **I John 1:9**. That does not involve "begging, pleading or asking" God to forgive you. You can cry bucket of tears, but until you do what the word says, it is not going to do anything but clear out your tear ducts. The scripture says, *"If we CONFESS our sins, He is faithful and just to forgive us our sins and to cleanse us from all unrighteousness."* (**I John 1:9 NKJV)**.

There are two instances that come to mind. David who said" **I acknowledged my sin to You, and my iniquity I did not hide. I said, I will confess my transgressions to the Lord [continually unfolding the past till all is told]—then You [instantly] forgave me the guilt and iniquity of my sin;"** (**Psalms 32:5 AMP)**. Confess and receive forgiveness. Secondly, there is the prodigal son who was a Jew that took his inheritance and left the family to go his own way. He finds himself feeding pigs and came to himself. He repented and came back home where his father received him in **Luke 15:12-24**. He confessed his sin, received forgiveness.

Have we misquoted this? We said repent and "ask God" to forgive you. No! We must be careful to say what God says and not what we heard someone else say what God said. He said confess the sin and He would be faithful to forgive and cleanse us. From there, forget it, and move on by faith that you are forgiven and cleansed. God does not remember your sins anymore; He forgot it. "**Their sins and lawless acts I will remember no more."** (Hebrews

17 NIV). Forgetting is a crucial step in this process. You must forget your past as well as forgive and forget what others have done to you. Oh, but I can't (you say). Oh, but you must if you want to be free from the past. Who are we to remember other people's sin? Let them go free so you can be free. Paul did and so can we.

Your past is forgiven and forgotten by God. There is no need to dig up, rehearse and hold onto past issues. It's not God that is reminding you of your past sins. It's the thoughts that you have not cast down and put under the blood of Jesus that are dogging you. Refuse to be held hostage by your past, take control of your thoughts. Renew your mind to what the word says and cast down the past thoughts according to 2 Corinthians 10:5. No one can do this for you but you.

Righteousness is having a clear conscience before God and a renewed mind that thinks like God thinks. God sees you through the eyes of Jesus Christ, as more than a conqueror, an overcomer, a royal priesthood, victorious. He sees you as a saint and not a sinner. Rehearsing and reliving your past gives you a sin conscience and it will prevent you from walking in victory. See yourself as a "saint" and not a sinner.

Paul emphasizes the fact that a man cannot be both saint and a sinner, nor holy and sinful, serving God and Satan. In his writings, he lays it out first as to why we are no longer sinners when we become born again and accept Jesus Christ. Pause and reflect on what the following scriptures are saying to us and see yourself as a "used to be sinner" and notice the past tense that he writes to the Romans. Paul writes:

"While we were (past tense) sinners, Christ died or us."

(Romans 5:8). *"Being therefore made free from sin, ye became servants of righteousness";* **(Romans 6:18)**. *"For when you were the servants of sin, you were free from righteousness."* **(Romans 6:20)**. *In other words Free from sin=Righteous, Serving sin=Sinner.*

Paul shows us in the following verses that we are to make a distinction between sinner and saints by identifying those called out as Christians. He is making it clear and letting them know that they are not to be labeled as sinners anymore but are now saints as he speaks to them saying:

"Among whom are ye also the called of Jesus Christ... called to be saints; "(Romans 1:6-7 KJV). To the church of God, which is at Corinth, *"...them that are sanctified in Christ Jesus, called to be saints (God's people)."* **(1 Corinthians 1:2 NKJV). "...let it not be once named among you as becometh saints" (Ephesians 5:3 KJV).** Saints –*"God's consecrated believers";* **(Hebrews 13:24 AMP).** *"...God's people – the* **saints (Revelations 5:8 AMP).** So, as believers in Jesus Christ we are now saints, not sinners.

I heard the words to a song that said, "A saint is just a sinner who fell down." That does not line up with God's perspective of us. What you choose to believe determines whether you can walk in that right place with God or not. Sinners do not walk in right standing with God because of their sinful, guilty, shameful mindset. I propose to you born-again saints of God, that you are righteous before God. You can come boldly into His presence and enjoy His presence free from your past and all condemnation. Come in like a priest, a king, a son, an heir...like you belong.

We are to be "established" in righteousness. Webster[18] defines established as made firm, stable. ***"In righteousness shalt thou be established; thou shalt be far from oppression, for thou shalt not fear and from terror; for it shalt not come near thee.*** **(Isaiah 54:14 KJV).** That is certainly good news. If you study the Psalms and Proverbs, you will be delighted to see the vast promises to the righteous. How do we get established? We do this by allowing the Holy Spirit to guide us in the reality of what Jesus Christ has already done for us by His death, burial and resurrection. We are to accept the victory He won for us. If you are constantly hearing teaching, preaching that keep you feeling condemned, you will remain in that mindset. E.W. Kenyon said, "The ministry has never realized that its work is to free man from sin consciousness and make him God conscious, son conscious, victor conscious, faith conscious and love conscious."[19] Let us rise up and take our place as VICTORIOUS SAINTS.

It is time for the manifestation of the sons of God who know their position as the righteous ones of God. These sons and daughters of God will show forth His glory by doing the greater works that Jesus spoke of.

To my fellow Saints, I pray for the confident, powerful mind of Christ to be established in you to walk and think in righteousness so that you can carry out His assignment in you. And Father, everyone who prays this prayer, bring them into a deeper intimacy with you because of their new confidence and boldness to come to you and receive in Jesus name.

Pray this in faith, believing you receive when you pray… Father, in the name of Jesus, I come before You and confess that I have held on to my past mistakes, my sins, my wrong deeds. You said in 1 John 1:9 that if we confess our sins, You are faithful and just to forgive us and cleanse us from all unrighteousness, so I come and confess now these sins I committed, (name whatever it is that is stuck to your memory). I am sorry for keep bringing up my past and for holding on to those things that I already brought up before and yet I still was troubled by these things. So now, I believe that You have forgiven me. I repent for letting condemnation, guilt and shame be more powerful in my mind than the power of the Blood of Jesus Christ that cleanses me and removes my sins from me. Father, I release everyone that I have held hostage in my mind, I forgive them, and I forget. I now receive my forgiveness by faith, I receive my cleansing and I thank you that I am now free in Jesus name. AMEN!

MINISTER SEREDA FOWLKES

Minister Sereda Y. Fowlkes is a native Virginian and was born in Crewe Virginia to the union of Earnest and Lottie Fowlkes (both deceased). She grew up on a small farm and learned to enjoy the harvest of fresh vegetables and fruit trees. She is the youngest of eleven children, seven girls and four boys. She learned to cook watching and tasting as her mother  showed her how to prepare food for the workers on the farm. She does not consider herself ready for an Iron Chef challenge, but she could stir up some tasty dishes if the need arises.

Sereda has been successful in the insurance industry for over 25 years and currently is the owner of Fowlkes Insurance Services, Inc. for the past 12 years. Sereda is also a distributor for Xango –a natural juice supplement for wellness. She is passionate about ministering healing to those who have not known the good news that healing is a benefit of salvation. Minister Fowlkes was introduced to H. J. Hines Ministries where she has received much of her foundation and development in the spiritual gifts. Sereda flows prophetically in tongues, interpretation of tongues and prophecy, and serves as an intercessory prayer.

She is a member of Family Worship Center DC, a Pentecostal church where she serves on the Altar ministry, Welcome team and Information ministry. She is also serving as a financial team member and assists in Pastoral support.

Sereda is passionate about bringing the truth to the lost and to other Christians that have not walked in the benefits of the authority of the believers. She is an exhorter and encourager to those who seem to have lost the light of the glorious gospel. She believes that quitting is not an option, because the back of the book says we "OVERCAME by the BLOOD of the LAMB."

CHAPTER 4

Call Me Righteous

It was no good that I've done
To make You call me one of Your sons
Couldn't pay the price to save my life
But You took the cost, and brought back what was lost
Now You call me righteous, since You changed my nature
Call me righteous, changed my name
Call me righteous, I'm a brand new creature
Call me righteous, I'm not the same.[20]

I grew up with some vague definition of righteousness that made the possibility of obtaining it appear to be impossible. Righteousness was defined by a particular style of dress. The definition even included standards for the correct way to style, color and *not* cut one's hair. There were stipulations regarding the use of make-up and a list of events and activities one could not participate in. I remember going to church one night after having just washed my hair. I had combed it out into an afro. One of the church mothers approached me and asked me if I was still saved. That night I discovered that the older church members thought you could lose your righteousness from one day to the next just by changing your hairstyle, painting your nails, or going to a basketball game.

Righteousness is a gift we receive from God. All we have to do to receive this gift is to accept it by faith. When we put our faith in Jesus and recognize that He is the one who paid the penalty for our sins, God then names us righteous. The righteousness of Jesus was paid on our account and we are righteous in the sight of God. We must first repent from our past sins so that we will be clothed in the righteousness of Jesus Christ **(I John 1:9 and Isaiah 61:10)**. In order to repent, we must humble ourselves before God, pray, seek after Him with our whole hearts, and turn away from our sinful ways. *"If my people, which are called by my name, shall humble themselves, and pray, and seek my face, and turn from their wicked ways; then will I hear from heaven, and will forgive their sin, and will heal their land"* **(2 Chronicles 7:14 KJV)**. God wants us to pray with fervent, effectual prayers so that even the gates of hell cannot prevail **(James 5:16, Matthew 16:18-19)**. It is this kind of praying that will change lives and bring breakthrough.

Righteousness is God's standard. It is His way of behaving, His character. Everything God says and does is right. We are spiritually right with God because of Jesus when we accept Him as our Lord and Savior. We are not righteous because we wear no jewelry, have memorized the entire book of Psalms and do not attend football games. If we could live right every waking hour and even dream right dreams, we could still never declare that we are righteous just because we live a good life. We can sing in the choir, serve on many church boards, and usher on Sundays, but we can still never declare that we are righteous were it not for the fact that Jesus shed His blood on Calvary on our behalf. Every sin that we could ever commit was placed on Jesus when He went to the cross. It was there that our sins were laid to rest. All the sin of Man was placed upon Jesus. He was the only one who could make this sacrifice, because He had the power to lay down His life and then pick it back up again.

When Jesus died, our guilt and condemnation died and Righteousness came alive. We now wear the righteousness of Jesus as a breastplate to protect us against the devices of the enemy. *"For he put on righteousness as a breastplate..."* (Isaiah 59:17 KJV). *"Stand therefore...having on the breastplate of righteousness"* (Ephesians 6:14 KJV).

When we receive Jesus as our Lord and Savior, we can place our past sins where they belong, in the past. We can then focus on our right standing with God. Although God convicts us of past sins, He never condemns us. Satan will try to make us feel guilty, ashamed, condemned and even hopeless when we sin. He does his best to make us feel unworthy so we will lose our confidence and never approach God to receive His forgiveness and answers to our prayers.

We have a tendency to reject the fact that we are righteous in God's eyes. Instead, we focus on our sins. Just as doing good things for others will not make us Christians, neither will doing bad things against others cause us to no longer believe in Jesus. We just need to focus on righteousness rather than our sins. As long as we are focused on righteousness, we will find it difficult to continue sinning because we soon realize that we have no righteousness of our own. It is all about Jesus making it possible to be called righteous. When we are called righteous, our love for the Master will help us to want to live holy, clean lives.

For example, Bill went to Mr. Jones asking if he could have some money. It was a huge sum of money that he asked for. He had gotten over his head in debt and then lost his job. It was not because of any emergency or life crisis. He made some poor money decisions and had very bad work habits. Mr. Jones had no special reason to give this young man any money, but he gave it to him. Bill did not deserve it and Mr. Jones did not have any duty to give it to him, but he did and paid all of Bill's debt. As far as his creditors were concerned, Bill was officially debt-free. He was bankrupt, broke, penniless, tapped out, but still had no debt. I am certainly not comparing this small act to that of Jesus. I am merely using this as an illustration. Mr. Jones paid a debt that he did not owe so Bill could be called debt-free, even though he had no means to make himself debt-free. Jesus died on Calvary to pay a debt that He did not owe. So, we could be called righteous, even though we were sin-filled. Bill admired the life that Mr. Jones lived. He went on to become financially independent because he decided to emulate Mr. Jones' financial prowess.

Through one man's (Adam) sin, we all became sinful; however, through one man's (Jesus) act of righteousness, we all have right standing with God **(Romans 5:12-20 AMP)**. It is through His righteousness that we are able to be free from condemnation, guilt, and sin. Were it not for the bloodshed of Jesus, we would still be held accountable for the sins we commit. This does not give us the right to keep on sinning. Even though we have all been made righteous, we still have to make an effort to live a good and righteous life and stay away from sin. *"And whatever we ask we receive from Him, because we keep His commandments and do those things that are pleasing in His sight"* **(I John 3:22 KJV)**. We give our lives to Christ and allow His image to shine through us in our deeds.

It is then that we can bear the fruit of righteousness. *"Being filled with the fruits of righteousness, which are by Jesus Christ, unto the glory and praise of God"* **(Philippians 1:11 KJV)**. This fruit allows us to make right decisions, saying and doing the right things.

Let me make one thing very clear. God rains on the just as well as the unjust **(Matthew 5:45)**. Even when we do not live righteous lives, our prayers can still be answered, because were it not for the blood of Jesus being shed on our behalf, we could not claim righteousness as ours **(II Corinthians 5:21)**. It is His righteousness. He shed His blood so we could have it as ours. We are not born righteous. God changes our nature and calls us righteous. As Fred Hammond sang, there was nothing good that we have done to make ourselves righteous. Even Jesus acknowledged that the only good One is God Himself. *"And Jesus said unto him, 'Why callest thou me good? None is good, save one, that is, God'"* **(Luke 18:19 KJV)**. We are not made righteous by what we have done, because none of us is perfect. He calls us RIGHTEOUS. *"But we are all as an unclean thing, and all our righteousnesses are as filthy rags"* **(Isaiah 64:6 KJV)**. Because we serve a graceful and merciful God, He places our sins into a sea of forgetfulness. *"How far has the Lord taken our sins from us? Farther than the distance from east to west!"* **(Psalm 103:12 Contemporary English Version CEV)**.

The following actions can be taken to allow us to take full advantage of God's gift of righteousness:

Repentance - Walking in righteousness does not mean that we will never sin or make any mistakes. If we fall in sin, we must quickly confess our sin and repent.

"My little children, these things write I unto you, that ye sin not. And if any man sin, we have an advocate with the Father, Jesus Christ the righteous" **(I John 2:1 KJV).**

Relationship - We must develop a relationship with the Father by spending time in the Word, praying, and then doing the Word. *"Henceforth I call you not servants...but I have called you friends; for all things that I have heard of my Father I have made known unto you"* **(John 15:15 KJV— See verses 1-15).**

Rhema - We must study the Word if we are to grow in Christ and obey His commands. A Rhema Word is a "now" word that is applied to a current situation, perhaps a prophetic utterance. *"All scripture is given by inspiration of God, and is profitable for doctrine, for reproof, for correction, for instruction in righteousness"* **(II Timothy 3:16 KJV).**

Rest - When we receive His righteousness as our own, we can find rest for our souls. *"He maketh me to lie down in green pastures: he leadeth me beside the still waters"* **(Psalm 23:2 KJV).** *"Come unto me...and I will give you rest"* **(Matthew 11:28 KJV).**

Rewards - Some of these rewards are: eternal life (**Titus 3:4-7**), restoration (**Psalm. 3**), protection (**Psalm 91**), boldness (**Proverbs 28:1**), and answered prayer (**James 5:16**). Many more rewards are outlined for the righteous in the Word! *"He that...receiveth a righteous man in the name of a righteous man shall receive a righteous man's reward"* (**Matthew 10:41 KJV**). *"He brought me forth also into a large place; he delivered me, because he delighted in me. The L*ORD *rewarded me according to my righteousness; according to the cleanness of my hands hath he recompensed me. For I have kept the ways of the L*ORD*, and have not wickedly departed from my God"* (**Psalm 18:19-21 KJV**).

We are to strive to be righteous just as He is righteous! We are to be holy just as He is holy. Come as you are, but do not stay that way. God loves us so much that He called us RIGHTEOUS. If we want our effectual, fervent prayers to avail much and our lives to be victorious in Christ, we will accept God's free gift of righteousness by faith in Jesus. Call *me* Righteous.

PRAYER

Father God,

We thank You for sending Jesus to be offered in our stead so that we could be called Righteous. Thank You for the ultimate sacrifice of love You made for us. Thank You for choosing us as Your own that we can be holy (consecrated and set apart) for You. I pray for my brothers and sisters that they will accept the gift of righteousness that You freely give to us so that we may reap the bountiful rewards.

I pray that we will strive to live righteous lives, knowing that this will directly affect our prayers when we pray fervently and effectually. We pray that You give us clean hearts and clean hands that we might live lives that are pleasing in your sight. We pray for clean thoughts, knowing that as we think, so we are. We pray for surrender, that we will not yield our bodies to sin, but instead offer ourselves to You as instruments of righteousness. We lift Your people and our families to You that You may get the glory out of our lives. Send fresh anointing on our lives and in our homes that Your purposes may be fulfilled. We pray for a hot pursuit of Your presence and that Your children will chase after You until we find You. We thank You for dying in our stead that we may be called Righteous. We have come to you as we are, but we thank You in advance for not leaving us that way. We anxiously await with great expectation the blessings You have ordained for our lives. Thank You in advance for Your answers. Nevertheless, not our will, but Yours, be done on earth in our lives as it is in heaven. In the name of Your Son, Jesus, we pray. Amen and so be it!

DEBORAH SILVER ADAMS

Deborah Silver Adams (Sister Debbie) has lived in the Fredericksburg, Virginia, area most of her life. This Preacher's Kid (P.K.) has served as praise and worship singer, prayer intercessor, children's church leader, choir director, newsletter editor, Sunday school instructor, Vacation Bible School  director, youth leader, secretary, and financial secretary. She has initiated programs, trained leaders, and then turned operations over to others to lead and maintain.

A member of Temple of Deliverance (Mineral, Virginia) most of her life, she also attended Land of Promise Church (Spotsylvania, Virginia), and Tower of Deliverance (Fredericksburg, Virginia). God also allowed her to connect with Sisters of the Son and Kingdom Community Outreach Ministries.

She has been married to her high school sweetheart Tyrone Adams, Sr., for 33 years, and they are the proud parents of three children, Ty, Robin and Justin, a daughter-in-law, a son-in-law, and 7 grandchildren. Employed as a bookkeeper and personal care assistant, she is currently pursuing her degree in business management through the Virginia Community College System.

CHAPTER 5

Effectual Prayer

Effectual prayer is the prayer that produces or is able to produce a desired effect. It is the prayer that is fruitful, operative, productive, and effective. This prayer is offered with conviction, focus and devotion based on the word of God. In the Lord's Prayer, we are taught that the will of God ought to be done on earth as it is in heaven. When Jesus gave us authority to tread upon serpents and scorpions according to Luke 10:19, He was indeed provoking us to be vigilant as God's official legislatures here on earth. He was giving us the power to stop the work of the devil where we dwell. We cannot afford to standby when illegal stuff goes on unchecked where we have dominion **(Genesis 1:28)**. It is our responsibility to enforce the will of God here on earth.

In Exodus 32 and 33, Moses demonstrates what we can call effectual prayer. Israel has sinned before God and God was annoyed to the level that? He wants to wipe them out of existence and make Moses a new nation for him to lead to the Promised Land. Moses begins by reminding God of His covenant with Abraham, Isaac, and Jacob. **(Exodus 32:13)**. When we stand on the word of God as we pray, we are praying in the will of God. God is obligated to do what His word says because He has magnified His word above His entire name **(Psalms 138:2)**. He follows His word to perform it. He says in **Isaiah 45:11b (KJV)** that *"Concerning the work of my hands command ye me."* This means that we have to make it a habit to read the scripture and to pray using the scripture. The angels only execute the prayer that is word based. They wait to hear the word of God in our prayers because that is the language they understand. It follows that even if we pray eloquently without using the word of God, the angels have no assignment to execute because they are yet to hear a command. *"Bless the Lord you His angels, who excel in strength, who do His word, heeding the voice of His word"* **(Psalms 103:20)**. At the end of this chapter, I will pen down a sample, prayer that is word based that can help us pray according to scripture as believers.

Effectual prayer demands that we get out of the familiar place. God will always withdraw us to Himself when He wants to speak to us. Going on a retreat to seek the face of God is a very healthy practice. Intimacy demands presence. In the natural, we build relationships spending time with those we love. The same is applicable with God. The more we spend time with Him the more we build an intimate relationship with Him. God cannot reveal to us the secrets of His presence when we do not want to spent time with Him. When Moses was interceding for the children of Israel after they had made and worshiped the golden calf, he pitched a tabernacle outside the camp meeting and called it, "the tabernacle of meeting" **(Exodus 33:7)**. Everyone who desired to seek the Lord was expected to go out of the camp into the tabernacle of meeting. However, the children of Israel did not take advantage of this tabernacle to establish a personal relationship with God. Rather, they stood at the doors of their tents and watched Moses go into the tabernacle to meet with God. It is only Joshua who got the revelation of the presence of God and lingered in the tabernacle. It is not surprising that he got the spillover of the anointing and eventually received the mantle to take over from Moses. There has to be some shifting if we want to hear the voice of God. We cannot remain in our comfort zones and expect God to move in our lives.

Effectual prayer is also selfless. It puts the needs of others before our own needs. Moses gives us a very good example in Exodus 32:11. God was ready to consume them and make for Moses another great nation to lead; but Moses pleaded on their behalf until God relented. Even though the Israelites had annoyed Moses on several occasions, he still put their need before his own need. He did not take pleasure in the fact that God could destroy them; rather, he interceded for them. He even asks God to consider that they are His people (Exodus 33:13b). This shows that Moses was very selfless in his intercession. When we look at the perversion in the society that we live in and how people have strayed from the saving grace of the Lord, we need to look at them with compassion because the god of this world has blinded their minds **(II Corinthians 4:4 KJV)**. We need to selflessly intercede for them that their chains be loosed.

Effectual prayer is released from the foundation of the rock, Jesus. God told Moses, *"There is a place by me, and you shall stand on the rock."* **(Exodus 33:21 KJV).** *"So it shall be, while my glory passes by, that I will put you in the cleft of the rock, and will cover you with my hand while I pass by."* **(Exodus 33:22 KJV).** Jesus is the Rock of Ages. He has been given the name that is above every other name.

He is our refuge and our stronghold. His name is a strong tower, we run to it, and we are safe. As believers, we are snipers in the realm of the spirit. Our vantage position is on the Rock- Jesus. It is from this default position that we are able to access all that God has ordained for us. When we put on the whole armor of God that we use to offensively attack the enemy, our standpoint is the Rock, Jesus. The armor is charged with the anointing that comes from the Rock. The belt of truth derives its grip from Jesus- the Way, the Truth, and the Life. The shield of faith has its anchorage on the Rock. This shield fortifies because Jesus is the shelter in the time of storm. The breastplate of righteousness, whose source is the Rock, conceals our individual righteousness that is as filthy rags. The helmet of salvation covers our minds from being polluted by the false splendor that the world offers. The mind is renewed because the Rock releases a renewal. The feet are firm on the Rock, which is the firm foundation. We cannot walk in error. His word illuminates our path and gives us direction on where to go.

"The kingdom of God is not meat and drink but righteousness peace and joy in the Holy Ghost." **(Romans 14:17 KJV)**. The kingdom of God is established on righteousness; however, it is not our righteousness but the righteousness of Jesus. *"A child will be born to us, a son will be given to us, and the government will rest on his shoulders... on the throne of David and over his kingdom, to establish it and uphold it with justice and righteousness..."* **(Isaiah 9:6-7 New American Standard NAS)**. When we go before the Lord in prayer, what qualifies us to access His presence is the righteousness of Jesus. God looks at the mark of the blood of His son. Therefore, we go before Him in

adoration exalting Jesus for becoming our righteousness. *"Seek ye first the kingdom of God and his righteousness and all these things shall be added to you."* (Matthew 6:33 KJV). Jesus is God's righteousness. It means that righteousness is something to be sought for; it is something to be pursued. We must reach a level where our thoughts are arrested and our entire system is yielded to the Spirit of God. There has to reach a moment when we are panting for the presence of the Lord like David in Psalms 63:1-2. This has nothing to do with how smooth the going is; pursuing God is independent of the circumstances that we are going through. In the natural, we spend time in the gym to work out our muscles so that we remain physically fit. In the realm of the spirit, faith is a muscle that needs to be worked out and our work out station is our prayer closet. When we spend time in prayer and reading the word, we build our faith in God. Faith is the hand that receives what God has promised in His word.

In my pursuit for God, I have come to learn that the word of God is food indeed. It is the one that makes our faith to grow. However, this food must have a base on which it can be served for effective consumption. You cannot have an effective prayer life without a foundation. Faith has the ability to grow when it is fed with the right diet. When you are clothed with the righteousness of Jesus Christ that comes through faith, you are able to feed your faith without condemnation. *"There is therefore now no condemnation to those who are in Christ Jesus, who don't walk according to the flesh, but according to the spirit."* (Romans 8:1 KJV). This means that when we receive Jesus in our lives we are delivered from condemnation because He clothes us with His righteousness.

Our faith begins to grow as we yield ourselves to His word. Transformation through the word comes by choice. That is why two people can receive Jesus the same day but when you check their level of maturity a year later there will be a difference depending on what material each has used to build on the foundation that was laid by Jesus Christ.

FASTING

Effectual prayer is also perfected through fasting. Fasting is when we deprive the body of what it likes in order to desensitize it and make the spirit alert. Food makes the body active but numbs the spirit. The opposite is also true. Fasting is the avenue that God uses to increase our spiritual sensitivity to His will. Divine assignments become clearer when we are fasting. We are able to hear God with clarity because we are not distracted.

We download the oracles of God with ease; unbelief is killed during this time, doubt is subdued; and all the loud noises within our surrounding that would otherwise bring unbelief are silenced. This is the time we remain facing the mercy seat unhindered. When the disciples were defeated to cast out a dumb spirit from a boy, his father of was very frustrated. He waited for Jesus to come and desperately narrated the ordeal. Jesus cast the foul spirit from the boy and he was delivered. However, the disciples wanted to know why they could not perform that task. Jesus told them *"This kind can come out by nothing but by prayer and fasting"* (Mark 9:29 KJV). This means that fasting destroys unbelief. Jesus never made fasting optional, it is actually mandatory for every believer that is why He said, "when you fast" and not "if you fast" (**Matthew 6:16**).

John was told, "***Come up here and I will show you things that must be hereafter.***" **(Revelation 4:1 KJV)** When we hear that Lord say "Come up here," He requires a paradigm shift from us. This is not a moment to reason, nor to rationalize, it is a moment of obedience and action.

That means that where John was prior to that was a place of defeat, a place of failure, a place of complacency, a place of compromise. The Lord had to call him up; he had to be elevated. He had to be removed from the ordinary familiar place in order to be able to see and to hear what God was going to reveal. So many things had caused him to be blindfolded. First, he had been banished to the isle of Patmos, a place of loneliness. He may have had moments of self-pity and hence he needed some reassurance. The Lord had to ask him to come up.

Over twenty years ago, my cousin and I set aside a weekend to seek God in prayer and fasting. We started praying on Friday night into Saturday. On Saturday afternoon, I saw a vision. In the vision, there were hundreds of white sheep in a large meadow feeding. The plain was vast and beautiful. Then a light shone in the horizon and a shepherd came walking gracefully with a long rod in his hand towards me. He extended his arms towards me and an open bible appeared from nowhere and landed before me. In that open bible, there were two keys. The man pointed at the bible and then pointed at the sheep. He never spoke a word to me. I stretched my hand and took the bible. I did not know that I had received a visitation from the Lord. I was so scared but later I came to learn that I had the calling of God upon my life. I was told that this calling had to be birthed in prayer because the devil will always fight our destiny to abort what God has planned. God has raised me to become an intercessor over the years and to impart the same gift in others. I have seen God raise up prayer warriors.

PRAYER

My father and my God, I come before your holy throne in the matchless name of Jesus, Savior and Lord of my life. I thank you for the blood of Jesus that qualifies me to have access into your presence. I honor you for who you are. You have given me boldness to enter the holiest by the blood of Jesus according to **Hebrews 10:19**. Therefore, I am free from every trace of condemnation because of your completed work at Calvary. I command my soul to bless you Lord, and all that is within me blesses your holy name. You are the one who forgives my iniquities; you heal all my diseases, you redeem my heart from destruction and you crown me with loving kindness and tender mercies. May your name be magnified. I delight in dwelling in your secret place because it is only there that I can abide under your shadow. Thank You for your anointing that breaks every yoke. You have equipped me with weapons of warfare that are not carnal but are mighty in God to pull down strongholds. I declare and decree that I am a partaker of the blessings of Abraham. May those blessings locate me. Let your word that is a lamp to my feet; illuminate my pathway so that I do not walk in error. May the spirit of wisdom be my portion in all the decisions that I make today, in the name of Jesus. Amen.

PASTOR JUDITH IMOITE

 I came to know the Lord in the year 1984 when I was in high school in Kenya. I graduated from high school got trained as a teacher and taught at three different high schools between the years 1989 and 2008 in Kenya.

Within my 18 years of teaching, the Lord enabled me to mentor and nurture many teenagers some of who have grown to be great ministers of the gospel. I got married in 1989 to Bishop Imoite Papa and I am a mother of four, 3 sons and a daughter. I was ordained Pastor in July 2007 the same time my husband was consecrated Bishop. I came to the United States in the fall of 2008 to pursue a Doctorate in Educational Administration and Policy in Howard University, DC.

By the grace of God, I will be graduating in December 2013. I currently serve at Bethel World Outreach Church in Silver Spring, MD where the Lord has enabled me to raise intercessors for the kingdom. I operate in the teaching and intercession ministry. I believe that nothing can withstand the force of prayer.

CHAPTER 6

Righteousness

The word righteousness derives from a root word, meaning "straightness." It simply means living upright or holistic living according to God's standards. One of the chief attributes of God is righteousness. God's character, who He is, exhibits the force of all righteousness. Because of that, in Him, we are made righteous. Not because of inherently good works, but because of faith in Him who heals and forgives. Let's face it: we have all sinned and fallen short of God's glorious standards. **(Romans 3:23 KJV)**. Yet God with undeserved kindness declares us righteous! Since the fall of man in the Garden of Eden, man inherently became unrighteous. His sinful act alienated him from the Father of righteousness. Although one may be morally good, his or her deeds alone, does not merit them righteous. The redemptive blood of Jesus the Christ alone makes us righteous. Our righteousness alone is as filthy rags **(Isaiah 64:6 KJV)**. However, we are made clean when we accept Yeshua because in Him is pure righteousness. Hallelujah! No more turtledoves or sacrificing of bullocks. The Savior of the world, the sacrificial lamb ultimate death on the cross, was an outward demonstration and love of His righteousness to all mankind. Regardless of the state of man, Jesus is the same yesterday, today, and forever **(Hebrew 13:8 KJV)**.

He has an unchangeable priesthood.

Many believers have a construed perception and interpretation of the meaning of righteousness. For many it hinges on the belief that if one were to become righteous, it was contingent upon what they did or did not do. In other words, contrary to that belief, crossing every "t", dotting every "I", seeing no evil, thinking no evil, making no mistakes, and being judgmental of those that do makes one *self*-righteous. Jesus is our perfect example and the exemplary model of righteousness. ***"And be found in him, not having mine own righteousness, which is of the law, but that which is through the faith of Christ, the righteousness which is of God by faith."*** **(Philippians 3:9 KJV)**. Jesus exhibited love to all. The Samaritan woman at the well, the woman caught in the act of adultery, the thief on the cross, the mentally disturbed man in the tomb, you and me are all recipients of the grace and righteousness of God. Jesus always brought healing, deliverance, peace, and calm to all that called on His name. Will you call on His name today and experience His relentless love for you? His righteousness is available to you.

RIGHTEOUS IN ACTIONS

How deep is the Fathers love for you? It amazes me each time I read about the woman caught in the very act of adultery. Was she guilty? Yes! Was it custom to stone a woman caught committing such an abominable act? Absolutely yes! The religious leaders gathered their stones raged and indignant, sitting in the seat of judgment, they prepared to stone this woman. They deemed themselves righteous by a judgment of their very own. None of them were justified in stoning her because they were in and of themselves with sin and *self*-righteous! Moreover, Jesus knew all of them had skeletons in their closets! He boldly proclaimed this declaration "He that is without sin, cast the first stone." They all one by one dropped their stones. Some in guilt, some in shame, yet all knowing that the last one standing before the adulterous broken -hearted woman was Holy and His righteousness superseded the righteousness of any man. All power belongs to God to save all, heal all, deliver all and set all free. Hallelujah.

RIGHTEOUS IN DEEDS

"And His righteousness endures forever." **(Psalms 111:3 KJV).** Just like the thief on the cross, situations and circumstances sometimes arise at a pivotal time in life that only a Sovereign God ultimately has the final answer concerning the fate and outcome. He deposited in man

the need to need Him. When all else and others fail there is an urgency in all of us to seek and knock and plead for God's mercy and favor. The thief hanging on a cross-hopeless, deserving death according to the law recognized that he needed a savior. Just like us, deserving death but God's mercy paid the penalty for our unrighteousness. Jesus, the King of Kings, hanging on the cross beside him, forgives him of his selfish deeds and acts as a thief and says to him, "This day, you will be with me in paradise." Oh, what love! It was evident the man was guilty and lived a life of unrighteousness and had no works to follow him. Nevertheless, Christ received him unto Himself and welcomed him in His Kingdom. Oh, happy day! Jesus laid down His life and the thief received everlasting life. No one will ever love you, care for you, know everything about you and still love you like Jesus the Father of righteousness.

RIGHTEOUS AND THOUGHTS

"For I know the thoughts I think towards you, thoughts of peace not evil to give you an expected end." **(Jeremiah 29:11 KJV)**. Forty-eight years ago before my father and mother came together, before conception; God began thinking righteous thoughts of me. In His mind, He mapped out the plan and purpose for my life. There were no stumbling blocks, detours, or delays that forfeited my destiny or His plan concerning my future. Before you were formed in your mother's womb, God knew your end from your beginning. Therefore, Christ Jesus sees you for who He has predestined you to be. May I encourage you by saying that God will take the ugly threads of your life and weave them into a beautiful pattern? God sees the best in you, thinks the best of you, and will love and bring you to your place of promise. Job said it best, "He knows the way that I take and when I am tried, I shall come forth as pure gold!" Not fool's gold, but pure gold!

SEVEN STEPS TO RIGHTEOUS LIVING

1.) Love others with genuine, pure, affection.
(Read I Corinthians 13:1-13)
2.) Take the lead in esteeming others more highly than yourself.
(Read Philippians 2:3)
3.) Bless those that persecute you. **(Read Matthew 5:11)**
4.) Do all that you can to live in peace with everyone. **(Read Romans 12:18)**

5.) Love the poor; walk humbly before God, having mercy. **(Read Micah 6:8)**

6.) Submit to governing authorities. **(Read Hebrews 13:7)**

7.) Help the poor. **(Read James 2:5)**

As you continue to seek the presence of the Lord, you will continually be empowered, transformed and conformed into His image. You will begin to see yourself in the image of your Heavenly Father. As you began to pray, ask the father to allow you to see yourself as He sees you, righteous in him.

PRAYER FOR RIGHTEOUSNESS

Heavenly Father, I worship You and glorify Your holy and righteous name. Father, Your word declares that if I seek first Your kingdom and righteousness I shall be filled, and all these other things will be added unto me. Father, add Your peace, Your love, and Your joy to my life. I declare and decree that I will walk in Your righteousness and truth. Continue to lead me in the path of righteousness, for Your namesake that I may dwell in your house forever in Jesus name... Amen.

OVERSEER FELICIA A. BILLUPS

 Overseer Felicia A. Billups is an anointed, gifted, and compassionate preacher, teacher, and counselor. She is Founder and CEO of Empowering Women Wisdom (EWW), a ministry designed to cultivate, empower, restore and encourage women from all walks of life in pursuing their God-given purpose and destiny.

She has been in ministry for over twenty years during which time she has traveled extensively throughout the United States as well as abroad. Her unique presentation has enabled her to minister to many denominations and organizations. Moreover, her gift has made room for her allowing her to minister at various women retreats and conferences, marriage seminars, youth conferences and crusades.

She is the wife of Chief Apostle William Billups who is the Presiding Prelate of Manifest Kingdom Global Alliance Inc. Overseer Billups serves as the National General Overseer. In her spare time, she enjoys reading, theater and cooking. She is the proud mother of five children, Tinisha, Darnell, Amariah, Alyssa and Gabriel.

CHAPTER 7

Robed In His Righteousness

One of the most important keys to effective prayer is the proper approach to God. I am not coming to you on the aspect of "coming boldly to the throne of grace" but a proper approach as it relates to your understanding. A place where the knowledge of God has been unfolded to you. You have embraced the knowledge that which you not only know, but also truly believe. To every believer in this hour who has ever within their heart desired for God to unfold to them the mystery of His Righteousness, let us take this journey together. My prayer is that the words that are written from this chapter will touch year heart so much that a supernatural experience will not only lift the words off the paper, but cause them to move through the atmosphere into your spiritual pores until they have consumed the borders of your heart. Your prayers unto God the Father will never be the same again! God wants us to embrace the knowledge that He unfolds to us that we may be robed in His Righteousness for our lives. It is also my desire that together we experience a joyous move of new authority and power that will cause us to shake a nation and awaken creation into her true destiny! We are the Sons of God who were created to manifest His Righteousness in the earth.

Bless us Father! Touch our hearts to see the unveiling mysteries of your Righteousness that we will from this movement forward never be the same again! Move us gently into the bosom of your existence. Let us dwell a moment Oh God, that this awaited time will not be lost, but remembered within our hearts forevermore, Amen!

There have been many who have spent countless hours discussing and dissecting the Righteousness of God through His Word. Throughout these discussions, there has been limited talk on exercising the Righteousness of God through Prayer. To everyone who has been called into the vocation of prayer there is no misunderstanding that this fact. No matter how determined you are to stand for Christ, to reach beyond the walls of mediocre and soar into higher heights and deeper depths, you will come to a crossroad! A moment in time where the understanding of your faith is unveiled and the need to truly embrace the Lord's Righteousness is before you. This is the place where your prayers meet their effectiveness and the question why if not, is raised.

In looking back on my life rehearsing the scenarios in my mind, I can remember carrying so much guilt and shame from the things that I had done (before the Lord and some in the Lord). Yes, I say that because they intertwine until there is a receiving of His Righteousness and an operation of His Righteousness in your life. I remember the pains of my failures, as if it was yesterday, and never understanding the guilt that continuously plagued my mind. I began to believe the guilt that I had built up and soon established patterns of defeat. Every time I tried to make a move, it was too far or not far enough! Every decision I thought to run with seemed to be at a backward pace. Failure had taken its own right to walk with me and possess the outcomes of my plans and actions. I had moved God completely out of the place of leading and guiding me continually in my life!

I had determined what a Righteous man was and uniquely enough the words that were spoken in my life were similarly teaching and molding me into a web of guilt, shame, and fear of God. Not the fear of His infinite wisdom and matchless being, but the fear of His wrath and judgment for the mistakes and failures I had made. Do you think that it is possible for a believer of God to obtain misinformation that can affect their whole course of life even though they wake up every morning with a desire to please God? From that moment forward because of the Lord's Righteousness, my life spun into a motion of un-webbing. It was the beginning of an unfolding of the His Righteousness and an understanding of every believer's call to rest in this position within Him. It was no longer enough for me to compromisingly slide by, but I had been called to SOAR and reach within me the deeper depths of His anointing. I was called to manifest His glory in the earth and it was because of His Righteousness that I would undoubtedly reach my promise.

Let's first be clear, there is no great mystery to the desire of man and his need to fulfill purpose. I am speaking of that which has been deposited within us to one day awaken and rise. Man was created with destiny locked inside of him. This is how a believer can be caught in an emotional slump of the mundane life and unexpectedly one-day experience a spiritual jolt that awakens the desire of their destiny. Greek theologians call it a "Kairos" moment in time, an opportune moment and opening where destiny moves through.

In prayer, there are no barriers or boundaries for the believer. When we understand, the Lord's Righteousness as it is robed upon us, there is nothing we cannot ask the Father nor is there anything we will not be able to do.

Our righteousness is as filthy rags. *"²For I bear them record that they have a zeal of God, but not according to knowledge. ³For they being ignorant of God's righteousness, and going about to establish their own righteousness, have not submitted themselves unto the righteousness of God. ⁴For Christ is the end of the law for righteousness to everyone that believeth. ⁵For Moses describeth the righteousness which is of the law. That the man which doeth those things shall live by them."* **(Romans 10:2-5 KJV)**. When we function in our own self- righteousness, we live within the same boundaries and barriers as well. When we continue to allow the force of our righteousness to rest upon us in our lives the works of love cannot prevail. Our righteousness judges man and condemns him into darkness separated from the Lord's forgiveness. Where there is a need to be strengthened in our righteousness, there is only room to weaken and alienate those who are believed to be helpless. Our righteousness determines the outcome of those who have fallen taking away their opportunity to rise and live again. God has given us an awesome gift that allows us to see beyond the here and now. *"⁶But the righteousness which is of faith speaketh on this wise, Say not in thine heart who shall ascend into heaven? ⁷Or who shall descend into the deep? ⁸But what saith it? The word is nigh thee, even in thy mouth, and in thy heart: that is, the* *word of faith, which we preach..."* **(Romans 10:6-8 KJV)**. Our righteousness rejects the faith of God and hinders the understanding of redemption from guilt and shame. When you pray within your own righteousness, your prayers are limited only to the things that man can do. Your prayers are based upon what you have seen and not what is believed, hitting a ceiling and becoming ineffective.

Who is this awesome God whose righteousness imputed our transgressions satisfying the law from which there would be a requirement of payment and judgment of our born state sin? His righteousness is to be without comparison to man who could never seal us as justified. He is the author of our faith in our redemption and the completion of our ability to believe. Within His righteousness, we are forever free from guilt and shame and are able to come boldly before the throne of grace, that we may obtain mercy, and find grace to help in time of need. **(Hebrews 4:16)**. In His righteousness we are given access and entitled to every benefit and reward. His righteousness secures our sanctification. Through the eyes of His righteousness, we are made perfect within Him. He who was perfect and we found no sin within Him **(II Corinthians 5:21)**, allowed Himself to be stretched upon the cross that He would be robed upon us with His Righteousness.

"I will greatly rejoice in the Lord, my soul shall be joyful in my God; for he hath clothed me with the garments of salvation, he hath covered me with the robe of righteousness, as a bridegroom decketh (himself) with ornaments, and as bride adorneth (herself) with her jewels." **(Isaiah 61:10 KJV)**. In the presence of the Father His righteousness upon us shines as treasures of His grace and beauty.

When we come and kneel before the Father in His righteousness His love moves through us for the healing and strength of others. We please the Father in our prayers not because of how we pray, but because we truly believe. Being robed in His righteousness means He covers our unrighteousness that it may exist no more. We are enveloped and covered with all of His goodness and virtues to be able to express them towards others in our prayers. We are a reflection of His goodness upon the earth because we have been redeemed from hand of the enemy. When we pray we must believe because we are the righteousness of God, the very expression of His great grace! We have been given access to the King's throne and granted the right to petition the Hand of God.

PRAYER

Father, as we kneel before you, covered in the robe of your Righteousness, we thank you for your love and grace given toward us. Thank you for making us righteous as we pursue you with our whole heart! It is our desire that we embrace the mantle of your Righteousness and allow it to possess our spirit that we are forever changed. Help us to understand our true position in the Righteousness of God. Help us to embrace within us the right to do the works of your Kingdome upon the earth. Every heart that desires to know you in a deeper and passionate way unveil your Righteousness to them that they may no longer respond separated from your love but as Sons of a living God who has given them access to His throne. Let them freely take upon your robe of Righteousness in acceptance to the finished work of your son Jesus Christ on the cross. Now Father every barrier, every wall, and limitation that stands before your people we pray for a holy boldness to rise up within them that breaks the bands of the enemy. We pray for a boldness that causes them to come into your presence with the assurance of your Word that dwells within them. We thank you for our confidence, which is in your son Christ Jesus. Father we bless your name and count it already done on the behalf of every believer. In the Name of Jesus the Christ we pray, Amen!

ELDER MONIQUE SIMMONS

 Monique is a prophetic intercessor and watchman warrior called to the end-time work of preparing a way for the coming third Great Awakening and Revival of the Church! She has been sent to charge an army of intercessors who will resume their position as watchmen and prophets. Monique is a "spirit-bearer" that causes the presence of God to hover over and rest upon the hearts of His people. She has been called to shift atmospheres with an igniting force of worship and praise. As a servant of the Lord, Monique has ministered the Word of the Lord during conferences, prophetic gatherings, and training sessions. She is a mentor who teaches the ministry of God's Kingdom and imparts understanding to the life and call of the believer, as well as, empowers and trains intercessors into the life and work of a watchman.

Monique received the indwelling and power of the Holy Spirit in August of 1993. In Monique's life, she has been graced by God to walk with prophetically profound mentors in the gospel gifted in the operation of powerful intercession, healing and deliverance.

She joins with many prayer generals in the body of Christ who minister the prophetic voice of God. Monique is a strong supporter of the continual prayer for Israel and the deliverance of the Messianic Jews. She is a member of her local assembly's

Intercessory Prayer Team at Kingdom Harvest Ministries in Landover, Maryland where Floyd E. Nelson, II, is Pastor. Monique has been called to work with pastors, who have been given by God according to His heart. She does this through providing prayer and support, which in turn she is able to see them being strengthened and empowered to finish the work! (Jeremiah 3:15) Monique resides in Maryland with her loving husband Vincent John Simmons, Sr., a wonderful intercessor and supporter, and her two children Viauna and Vincent John Jr.

VOLUME V - HOLINESS

TABLE OF CONTENTS

VOLUME V HOLINESS

CHAPTER 1

Be Ye

Holiness is the quality or state of being holy or sanctity. "Separation," or "setting apart," holiness is a general term to indicate sanctity, or separation from all that is sinful, impure, or morally imperfect; it denotes moral wholeness.

As believers, we need to be "set apart" from the world unto the Lord. We need to be living by God's standards, not the world's. God is not calling us to be perfect, but to be distinct from the world. *"But ye are a chosen generation, a royal priesthood, an holy nation, a peculiar people; that ye should shew forth the praises of him who hath called you out of darkness into his marvelous light"***(I Peter 2:9 KJV)**. This describes believers as "a holy nation." It is a fact! We are separated from the world. We need to live out that reality in our day-to-day lives, which Peter tells us how to do. *"¹³Submit yourselves to every ordinance of man for the Lord's sake: whether it be to the king, as supreme; ¹⁴Or unto governors, as unto them that are sent by him for the punishment of evildoers, and for the praise of them that do well. ¹⁵For so is the will of God, that with well doing ye may put to silence the ignorance of foolish men:*

¹⁶*As free, and not using your liberty for a cloke of maliciousness, but as the servants of God"* **(I Peter 2:13-16 KJV)**.

Holiness starts with a relationship with God. Be ye Holy as I am Holy, *"¹⁵But as he which hath called you is holy, so be ye holy in all manner of conversation; ¹⁶Because it is written, Be ye holy; for I am holy."* **(I Peter 1:15-16 KJV**). That is a command! As we grow in grace the knowledge of our Lord and Savior, we grow into an intimated fellowship with God. Only the born again children can live in holiness. I know you are thinking, "Oh, no not one of them that think you have to look holy to be holy. Appearance is a part of it. It is a mystery to anyone that is not in fellowship with God. Holiness flows from the heart of God.

Now since I have your attention let's expound on be ye Holy. Holiness separate us from the very nature of the world system, I did not say ISOLATE, which will cause anyone to be righteous. To be holy affects your very nature or inner man to do, say and look like the image of Jesus. You are incomplete as a true witness for Jesus without holiness. Holiness gives you access to God's presence. In the Spirit, you obtain power and authority to defeat the enemy. To be holy simply means you can live the abundant life in a corrupt world system. *"Follow peace with all men, and holiness, without which no man shall see the Lord."* **(Hebrews 12:14 KJV)**. You have a shield of protection as you walk in holiness. The word holy causes one to think it is impossible to be holy however, with understanding your duty to submit to the cleansing agent of the Spirit to make you holy. You cannot do it alone. God gives you the characteristic of Himself. Holiness is to be set apart indicating sanctity.

It is an attribute that causes you to stay free from bondage. Being morally stable constitutes a life style that the world will know you are different and Jesus is Lord of your life. It is important to humble yourself under the mighty hand of God to walk the walk God requires. Walking in Holiness will separate you from the lifestyle of the world. Being holy keeps you sensitive to the way of darkness. Holiness is a source of power that you choose in order not to sin.

Some are afraid of holiness, because holiness requires change. Yes, changes will be required. In order, to connect to the old man ways of living to be holy, you must change your look, behavior, conduct toward people and submission to God. We must change on both the inside and outside. It must start inward first. We have a relationship with the living God! We must daily live a set-apart life, not trying to "blend in" with the world, but instead living according to God's Word as we study the Bible and become a doer of His word.

Holiness will separate you from the lifestyle of the world to be holy keeps you sensitive to the way of darkness. Holiness has a source of power that will allow you to choose not to sin. Positional holiness is the result of what Christ did <u>for</u> us on the cross; practical holiness is the result of what the Holy Spirit does <u>within</u> us. Practical holiness is to be pursued by every believer. ***"For it is God which worketh in you both to will and to do of his good pleasure."* (Philippians 2:13 KJV).** However, verse 12 gives the balance: *"Work out your own salvation." "Wherefore, my beloved, as ye have always obeyed, not as in my presence only, but now much more in my absence, work out your own salvation with fear and trembling."* **(Philippians 2:12 KJV). (II Peter 1:2-4 KJV)** *"We have all things pertaining to life and godliness."*

However, verses 5 -7 give the balance: *"We supply diligence, moral excellence, knowledge, self-control, perseverance, godliness, brotherly kindness, and love."* **(II Peter 1:5-7)** *"Be transformed by the renewing of your mind."* **(Romans 12:2 KJV)**. However, verse 1 gives the balance: *"Present yourselves as living sacrifices (continually)."* **(Roman 12:2 KJV)**.

The Lord expect every believer to be holy, it becomes important for all Christians to submit themselves to God's total cleansing and impartation of perfect love. Isaiah said, *"Depart ye, depart ye, go ye out from thence, touch no unclean thing; go ye out of the midst of her; be ye clean, that bear the vessels of the LORD."* **(Isaiah 52:11 KJV)**. Therefore, *"Dearly beloved, let us cleanse ourselves from all filthiness of the flesh and spirit, perfecting holiness in the fear of God."* **(II Corinthians 7:1 KJV)**. We are to genuinely seek the face of the Lord, so that our whole spirit, soul and body will be preserved unto the coming of our Lord Jesus Christ. Is holiness (sanctification) necessary? YES! Our goal should always be to be separated to God in everything we do, not just in specific "holiness standards." After all God wants to live in us, so "Be Ye Holy".

H-Hunger	**Matthew 5:6**
O-Obedience	**Deuteronomy 30:1-2, 8-9**
L- Love	**Deuteronomy 30:16, 20**
I- Innocence	**Daniel 6:3-7, 23**
N-New heart	**Ezekiel 36:26-27**
E- Everlasting	**Romans 6:21-23**
S -Separation	**II Corinthians 6:16**
S- Seeking	**Matthew 6:33**

PRAYER FOR HIS KINGDOM

We come to You as humbly as we know how. Father, I confess my sins. You are faithful and just to forgive me my sins and to cleanse me from all unrighteousness. Jesus has been made unto me wisdom, righteousness, sanctification, and redemption.

I submit myself to You, Lord — spirit, soul, and body. I strip myself of my old, unrenewed self and put on the new nature, changing whatever needs to be changed in my life. The desire of my heart is to be a vessel unto honor, sanctified, fitting for the Master's use, and prepared for every good work.

Father, thank You for sanctifying me by the truth. Your Word is truth. Jesus, You consecrated Yourself for my sake, so I'll be truth-consecrated in my mission. In the name of Jesus, I repent and turn from my wicked ways. I wash myself, make myself clean. I cease to do evil, and I am learning to do right. In the name of Jesus my Savior, I pray. Amen.

MINISTER TONYA DEVILLE

Minister Tonya DeVille was ordained in 2012 and is currently a part of the ministerial staff of the Woman of God Ministries Inc. For the past three years, she has been under the leadership, mentorship and spiritual support of Overseer Trena Stephenson. Overseer Trena has been a tremendous blessing to Minister Tonya's life and spiritual foundation.

Minister Tonya was born on May 27 to Minister Regina Richmond and Melvin Roberson. She spent much of her formative years in Washington, D.C. Her parents instilled in Minister Tonya at an early age the importance of having a relationship with Christ. Being the child of a preacher, she spent a great deal of time in the church. With this solid foundation in Christ, Minister Tonya recognized the call of God on her life at an early age, 16. Minister Tonya's call comes from John 4:18-19, *"There is no fear in love; but perfect love casteth out fear; because fear hath torment. He that feareth is not made perfect in love. We love Him, because he first loved us."*

Minister Tonya confesses her belief and Trust in God and His word. She desires for you to worship the Father, spread the Gospel of Jesus Christ, His son, and to obey the Holy Spirit.

Minister Tonya received her formal education from Prince George's Community College. She received an Associates of Arts Degree in accounting. After completing this degree, Minister Tonya relocated to Atlanta, Georgia. During this short time in Atlanta, Minister Tonya felt like Abram, when God removed him from all of the familiar things in his life, for example, family, friends, and my surroundings. God was using this as a time of preparation. After a year, Minister Tonya relocated again to New Orleans, LA, where she would reside for almost five years. It was during this time that God began to use and prepare her to be an intercessor. Minister Tonya became a member of Second St. John Baptist Church, where she joined the mothers of the church for intercessor prayer. Minister Tonya is the mother of a beautiful talented, God-fearing daughter Karinton.

CHAPTER 2

The Law of the House Is Holiness

I believe that in order to have an effective prayer life, we must pursue a lifestyle of holiness. Holiness is the missing ingredient that is missing from the lives of many believers today within the Body of Christ.

"This is the law of the temple: The whole area surrounding the mountaintop is most holy. Behold, this is the law of the temple." (**Ezekiel 43:12 NKJV**).

This is the law of the house — From the top of the mountain on which it stands, to the bottom, all round about, all shall be holy. No buildings shall be erected in any part, nor place nor spot be appropriated to a common use. All shall be considered as being most holy.

I believe that house of which Ezekiel is talking about is typical of the   church of the living God. The church that is on earth is the only entity that can be called the house of God. The word tells us that God has chosen Zion as His holy habitation. The saints are built up as a spiritual house.

"[21]*in whom the whole building, being fitted together, <u>grows into a holy temple in the Lord,</u>*   [22]*in whom you also are*

built together for a dwelling place of God in the Spirit."
(Ephesians 2:21-22 NKJV).

"you also, as living stones, are being built up a spiritual house, a holy priesthood, to offer up spiritual sacrifices acceptable to God through Jesus Christ." **(I Peter 2:5 NKJV).**
We are being built together into a holy habitation of God through the Spirit. God resides in us according to the promise found in His Word.

And what agreement has the temple of God with idols? For youare the temple of the living God. As God has said: "I will dwell in them and walk among them. I will be their God, and they shall be My people." **(II Corinthians 6:16 NKJV).**

The church is the dwelling place of God. When I say church, I'm not talking about a physical building, but about the believers who make up the church, the ecclesia the called out ones. The church is the family of God and God the Great Father dwells in the midst of His people.

" ¹³For the Lord has chosen Zion; He has desired it for His dwelling place: ¹⁴This is My resting place forever; Here I will dwell, for I have desired it." **(Psalms 132:13-14 NKJV).**

"1His foundation is in the holy mountains. ²The Lord loves the gates of Zion, More than all the dwellings of Jacob."
(Psalm 87:1-2 NKJV). The church is God's house and therefore God provides for it as a man provides for his own home. He has spent His own strength for it exercising His wisdom on its behalf. He gave His only begotten Son for us, Jesus died for our sins and rose again.

God sent Jesus to rescue each one of from our sins.

"10And if Christ is in you, the body is dead because of sin, but the Spirit is life because of righteousness. 11But if the Spirit of Him who raised Jesus from the dead dwells in you, He who raised Christ from the dead will also give life to your mortal bodies through His Spirit who dwells in you." (Romans 8:10-11 NKJV).

"Therefore we were buried with Him through baptism into death that just as Christ was raised from the dead by the glory of the Father even so we also should walk in newness of life." (Romans 6:4 NKJV). We have been called to walk in the newness of life and that life is holiness.

"21What fruit did you have then in the things of which you are now ashamed? For the end of those things is death. 22But now having been set free from sin, and having become slaves of God, you have your fruit to holiness, and the end, everlasting life." (Romans 6:21-22 NKJV).

Church we who are in the Body of Christ must wake up to the reality that Christ has dealt sin a deathblow to sin on the cross. Therefore, it should not reign in our mortal body as the Apostle Paul stated in **Romans 6:12**. Now, that I have the foundation we need to recognize that God's house should not be lawless; in other words we should not be using our liberty in Christ to willfully commit sin. Our liberty in Christ is not a license to sin. We who dwell in the house of God are in God's immediate presence, and our ***"God is a consuming fire"*** (Hebrews 12:29 NKJV). He who dwells with the Father, Son and Holy Spirit the three in one God must be holy as well. In these last days, God is going to be sanctified in His people the church. Those who enter into the house of God in these last days and misbehave themselves; they are going to find that judgment begins at the house of God. How terrible are these word. Listen to what the Apostle Paul states in I Cor. 3:17. *"If anyone defiles the temple of God, God will destroy him. For the temple of God is holy, which temple you are."* **(1 Corinthians 3:17 NKJV)**.

These are some strong words from God to the Apostle Paul as he delivers it to the church of God. I pray today that the Holy Spirit will cause each us to understand and lead each of us to obey. The church of Jesus Christ must grow into Him. Ezekiel tells us in the text that upon the top of the mountain the whole limit thereof around about shall be most holy. Behold this is the law of the house. Every believer who makes up the House of God is called to be holy as the Lord our God is holy. Just what is the law of the house? I believe that the law of the house is purity, holiness, cleanness, righteousness, graciousness and God like. Everything that has to do with the Church of God must be holy. Here are the words" Upon the top the mountains the whole limit round about shall be most holy; observe again this scripture. It must be most holy! It must be most holy! In the old temple, there was only one chamber in the center that was most holy. This was called the holy of holies or the holiness of holiness. Today, in the church under the dispensation of Grace, every chamber, hall and court is to be most holy. The church is to be holy for we are representing a holy God here on the earth. Holiness is a lifestyle said the Lord that that is to be sought after by every believer in the church of God, that includes those who stand in the office of the five-fold ministry. Holiness is the character of God.

It is the desire of God that we the church be conformed into the image of His son. The Christian should be sanctified, "spirit, soul and body." *"Now may the God of peace Himself sanctify you completely; and may your whole spirit, soul, and body be preserved blameless at the coming of our Lord Jesus Christ."* **(I Thessalonians 5:23 NKJV).** We notice also in the text that holiness was to be conspicuous. We are not to be hidden in the valley or in the woods somewhere. However, Jesus stated in Matthew 5:14-16:

[14]"You are the light of the world. A city that is set on a hill cannot be hidden. [15]Nor do they light a lamp and put it under a basket, but on a lampstand, and it gives light to all who are in the house. [16]Let your light so shines before men, that they may see your good works and glorify your Father in heaven." **(Matthew 5:14-16 NKJV).** We are called to be God's peculiar people distinguished by the mark of holiness. The church of Jesus Christ is called to be a light like a city sitting upon a hill to give light to those in darkness. I pray to God that the true light of God begins to shine into this darkened world that is bound by sin. God has given us a standard and that standard is holiness.

Today in the church, we have those who want to take the shortcuts to get the power of God. Francis Frangipane stated that those who do that become frustrated at worse, a false teacher or prophet. There is tremendous power for us in God, but not without holiness. Holiness precedes power.[21] There will be a season of holiness that is coming to the body of Christ. I believe this is the generation that will see a new wave of holiness coming into the church, as we have never seen before. We are going to witness an end time outpouring of the Holy Spirit that is far greater than anything that you could ever imagine.

The world will witness the supernatural power of God through signs, wonders and miracles. They will witness the power of Jehovah God and know that He is one true and living God. A wave of holiness is always preceded by repentance. Please see the following scriptures and allow the Holy Spirit of God to minister to you:

"And it shall come to pass afterward That I will pour out My Spirit on all flesh; Your sons and your daughters shall prophesy, Your old men shall dream dreams, Your young men shall see visions." (Joel 2:28 NKJV).

Alas for the day! For the day of the Lord is at hand; it shall come as destruction from the Almighty. (Joel 1:15 NKJV).

"Blow the trumpet in Zion and sound an alarm in My holy mountain! Let all the inhabitants of the land tremble; for the day of the Lord is coming, for it is at hand:" (Joel 2:1 NKJV).

"The Lord gives voice before His army, for His camp is very great; for strong is the One who executes His word. For the day of the Lord is great and very terrible; who can endure it?" (Joel 2:11 NKJV).

"[12]Now, therefore," says the Lord, *"Turn to Me with all your heart With fasting, with weeping, and with mourning."* *[13]So rend your heart, and not your garments; Return to the Lord your God, For He is gracious and merciful, Slow to anger, and of great kindness; And He relents from doing harm."* (Joel 2:12-13 NKJV).

"[17]Let the priests, who minister to the Lord, Weep between the porch and the altar; Let them say, "Spare your people, O Lord, and don't give your heritage to reproach, that the nations should rule over them. Why should they say among

the peoples, Where is their God? ¹⁸Then the Lord will be zealous for His land, and pity His people." **(Joel 2:17-18 NKJV).**

Every major move or wave of the Holy Spirit has been preceded by a time of prayer and fasting. The outpouring of the Holy Spirit on the 120 gathered in the upper room was done by prayer, fasting and being in one accord. Azusa Street started because a handful of believer came together in one accord. God is calling forth in this hour to those who have an ear to hear what the Spirit is saying. He is calling for each us to get into His presence and stay on our faces before Him in repentance and intercession for the Body of Christ. A new wave of holiness, righteousness and consecration on a new level is coming to the Body of Christ, to prepare us for Christ coming.

There will be no more compromise or hypocrisy; emotionalism will be replaced by serious commitment and dedication. Do not be deceived church; Jesus is not coming back for a harlot bride that has been committing spiritual adultery with the world. He is not coming back for a bride that has become polluted with the sinful lusts and desires of this world. He is coming back for a holy end time remnant, a people who have been cleansed and purified without spot or blemish. Jesus came to this earth, suffered the shame, the agony of the cross, died, and was resurrected that we would be holy and without blemish. I know that you may be reading this and you don't think that it is impossible to live a holy life. The devil has lied to us and made us to think that living a life of holiness is not possible.

I pray that the world will get glimpse of the holiness of God as it is reflected through His church. Everyone should examine himself or herself to see if they are measuring up to the standard of God. We need to ask ourselves am I consecrated. Am I living up to God with my body, soul and spirit? Am I using the gifts talents and abilities that the Lord has given me for His glory? What am I living for? On the other hand, am I just living under the pretense of following God and only serving for my own selfish gratification? A good example is Ananias and Sapphire who pretended to give all and yet they kept back a part of the price. What are you holding back on to God? God desires that you give yourself fully unto Him, by living a holy consecrated, sanctified life. The law of the house is consecration, separation, obedience and holiness.

PRAYER

Lord Jesus, I gaze upon you by faith, and I believe that You are truly my sanctification and holiness. I believe You purify my heart by faith, and You break every bondage of sin. I take these words and cling to them, as I cling to you as my Savior. Amen.

PASTOR SAMUEL BURNS

 Samuel Burns is the Pastor and Founder of Bread of Life Full Gospel Church, located in Randallstown, Maryland. Pastor Burns favorite scripture that he has sought to live by is **Matthew 6:33.** *"Seek first the kingdom of God and His Righteousness. "*

Pastor Burns is married to Geraldine Burns aka (Geri). Pastor Burns and his wife Geri are the host of Victory Today Prayer Ministry heard each Saturday at 11 Am on Spirit 1400 AM in Baltimore. Pastor Burn's spiritual covering in the ministry is Apostle Aaron B. Claxton of Endtimes Ministries International. Pastor Burns also serves on the Board of Elders for World Evangelism, under the direction of Dr. Morris Cerullo.

Pastor Burn's greatest desire is to see the saints of God mature and reach their full potential in the Body of Christ.

CHAPTER 3

Dress In Holiness

"*Having therefore these promises, dearly beloved, let us cleanse ourselves from all filthiness of flesh and spirit, perfecting holiness in the fear of God* (**II Corinthians 7:1 KJV**). This verse alone says a lot. As Bill Burkett stated, "When we come to God, confessing our sins, the atoning blood of Jesus Christ forgives the past, washes the heart clean for the newly born child of God set off a chain of events in heaven that included a new name for the newly born child of God, an open line of communication between our prayer and the throne of God. Now holiness suddenly becomes our business. We are to take the initiative."[22]

The Holy Spirit will reveal the word of God to us and grace will teach us. However, we ourselves must execute the act of turning from the carnal way of life to the way of holiness, which pleases God. *"[11]For the grace of god that bringeth salvation hath appeared to all men. [12]Teaching us that denying ungodliness and worldly lusts, we should live soberly, righteously and godly in this present world."* (**Titus 2:11-12 KJV**). Holiness is both a positive and a negative process. *"[7]Submit you therefore to God. Resist the devil, and he will flee from you.*

⁸Draw nigh to God, and he will draw nigh to you. Cleanse your hands, ye sinners; and purity your hearts, ye double minded." **(James 4:7-8 KJV).** We see this principle demonstrated when the scripture tells us to "Resist the devil, and he will flee from you," and Draw nigh to God, and He will draw night to you."

It was resistance that caused Satan to leave Jesus after the wilderness temptation. This is an eternal foundation truth: to resist evil voluntarily must precede positive and lasting spiritual inflow. This is meeting the condition for the promised blessing.

We must understand what the word of God is saying about being holy. Holiness affects every area of our life. It is not the right language, our clothes or friends we chose, but when holiness is in the heart, it affects all these areas and much more. Holiness means to set apart. It's neither a man-made set of specifications or regulations. True holiness is the spirit of God and to know Him as the scriptures saith. Gods' love for us is unconditional with no string attached.

We need to grow in love with God. We need to get to know Him." *And this is life eternal, that they might know thee the only true God and Jesus Christ, whom thou hast sent."* **(John 17:3 KJV).** He has revealed Himself to us in His word and in our everyday personal lives. It is written that the Father has precious and exceedingly great promises for us. In our walk with the Father, we will have moments of not realizing where we are in our life. If you want more understanding and great intimacy with God, you must make reading God's Word, praying and seeking His face a priority in your life.

We take His Word and His life as a storybook. We read it repeatedly as a fairytale and never realize He is spirit. The words we read from the bible only provide a small portion of who He is. There are many hidden mysteries that He wants to reveal to us as we study and walk out His words. It's very important to establish and maintain a daily praying lifestyle with God in order to grow one's love for God. Prayer must not be neglected if you want your love for God to grow. Praying is a believer's armor against the enemies. *"Pray at all times (on every occasion, in every season) in the Spirit, with all (manner of) prayer and entreaty. To that end keep alert and watch with strong purpose and perseverance, interceding in behalf of all the saints (God's consecrated people)."* **(Ephesians 6:18 AMP)**.

We must follow Jesus as we study His life. We will find that Jesus constantly prayed. We should return to the Father to have an open communication with Him and to hear His instructions daily pertaining to His people and us. Jesus never missed His time with the Father. As sons and daughters of Christ, we should follow the relationship Jesus has with the Father; he is the only great example. The word of God and the Spirit of God cannot be measured; there is a realm of un-limitation. How will you ever know about Christ, if you can't find the time to seek His face in prayer? That which is divine cannot be measures by that which is human. You first must see you are spirit as Christ is Spirit. If you have not taken the time to even, make an effort to know God in his awesome power; then what is the purpose of thinking you are one with Christ?

How shall we achieve these goals of holiness? What we need is a love and power greater than the things we are rejecting. *"Set your affections on things above, not on things on the earth."* **(Colossians 3:2 KJV)**.

The love of Jesus is stronger than our carnal desires. The grace of God is greater than the power of sin. The only thing we want to know now is what can generate, or create this overpowering love and grace in our hearts, its prayer and going into His presence. When reading faithfully, it has a power much the same as prayer does when entered into with faith and purpose. It is the Father talking to us. The entrance of His Word, which gives light and understanding. The effects of sincere prayer life and reading His words are a deep and divine position in our lives, regardless of external circumstances.

In order to come into His presence we must know first that Christ welcomes our visits. He delights and embraces us when we come. It's as important to God as it is to us. Imagine getting up each day, putting on your favorite outfit, spraying on your favorite fragrance, making sure everything is in place just so someone special notice that you have taken the time to make a great personal impression. We tell ourselves in the mirror, that we look good. We get all dressed up hoping the object of your desire would whisper something into your ears. We should have this same attitude when we are dressing right toward the Father. All we have to do is come with a willing heart, with songs of praise and worship, showing God how much He is worth to us.

God could have any Angel in heaven, but He desires you. As I said earlier, holiness has nothing to do with friends we chose or our language. This is a relationship with the Father that causes us to want to move in the Father's will for our lives and others. The set apart causes us not to sin. Sin has no life; sin is anything that separates you from God. It could be envy, fear, un-forgiveness or anything that is out of the will of God is unholy.

Holiness does not just happen overnight; it is a process. As I said earlier, you must see the need to set yourself apart and flow in the will of the Father.

We have a free will to choose life or death. God spoke in His word to choose life. This simply means you can continue to follow your flesh and carnal mind, which leads to death, meaning separation from Christ. Choose life, which is eternal with the Father. It's not a hard thing to do but part of the problem is letting go of what feel good to your flesh. *"*[11]*For the grace of God that bringeth salvation hath appeared to all men*[12]*Teaching us that denying ungodliness and worldly lusts we should live soberly righteously and godly, in this present world."* **(Titus 2:11-12 KJV).** Any affection or lust that tends to turn us away from the Father must be reckoned as filthy and removed from our lives.

Word written by Bill Burkett says we are to "cleanse ourselves from all filthiness of the flesh."[23] Holiness is not a singular matter, but involves the whole being and the whole spectrum of life. Christians have the personal responsibility and the divine enablement to discipline his own body.

I want to share this with you hoping it will be a blessing to you because it was such an awesome day for me. In 1985, my mother shared with me her experience of making Jesus Christ, Lord of her life. It was a Friday evening, which was her normal day to go to choir rehearsal. On that day she said, she could not explain how or what made her detour from her direction to her church. She ended up at a holiness Pentecostal church. She could only remember that she was at the church altar repenting to God for all her sins on her knee. It wasn't because it was a holiness church, but it was God allowing her to make a great decision that day. She made a decision to choose Christ to be Lord over her life, at the age of 62 years old.

She told me, how great God had been to her. She told me she was going to continue into the past of righteous for God. I watched her change her lifestyle. She just started to read her bible, set-up a special time in morning and evening for devotions with God. Her conversation was always about how God was revealing Himself to her and how He was talking to her. She even expressed how we must keep ourselves set apart from all carnal thinking and sinful lust that she read in God's word. She passed away seven years ago. I can still hear her voice saying, "Don't let anyone or anything keep you away from God." Remember early in the chapter, I shared that we ourselves must execute the act of turning from the carnal way of life to the way of holiness, which pleases God. This is what we must do. We must put on our (Holy) garment and come into His presence daily, because He is waiting on us. If you have anything that would separate your relationship with God, please don't wait, be smart get an intimate relationship with the Father so you can be dressed right, which is holiness; because He is holy. Our God is holy! In closing, I would like to leave with you a prayer that you may pray as you journey through your walk into holiness.

Father:

I come before You first with a repentance heart. If there is anything I said or have done today, I asked that You forgive me. I pray that we walk in Your will for our lives. I pray for holiness that we don't forget that You are holy and if I am in You than I must be holy. God I pray that the word of God would watch over our lives and that it would cleanse us from all filthiness of the flesh. Remove the memories that would try to keep us in the past. Help us to forget the things of the past and move into a Kingdom mindset of righteousness, peace, and joy in the Holy Spirit because that is what Your word says. I pray for more souls to come into the Kingdom. I pray that Jesus is moving on our behalf to bring every blessing and manifestation of every promise of the Father. I pray that we are the Son of God, and it doth not yet appear what we shall be; but we know that we shall be like Him (God), for we shall see Him as He is. I pray a guard over our hearts, spirit and our minds let not the enemy sow seed of discouragement, frustration, anger, deceit, fear and unbelief in Jesus name. Amen.

PASTOR ANGELA BRADLEY

Angela Bradley is Pastor of The Plan Ministries, under the leadership of Apostle Carnal Bradley, her loving husband and Founder/Overseer of the ministry. Angela has a tremendous passion for God Word coupled with a love for God's people. She has a contagious spirit of generosity that flows through every faucet of her ministry. Her vision is uncompromisingly clear, with one central principle; to build and develop a Kingdom of empowered people for the Kingdom of God that they may establish a pure personal relationship with God.

Pastor Angela has been serving God's people for over forty years, with nineteen years at Freedom Church in Forestville, Maryland, under the leadership of Pastor Robert Whittaker (deceased) and Pastor Eric Yarbrough serving as an usher and teacher, but most remembered as an awesome servant to God's people.

In addition to her current role in May 2002, Pastor Angela was ordained as a prophet at Keys to the Kingdom Ministries International Fellowship, under the leadership of Bishop Kenneth D. Grimble in Augusta, Georgia. In August 2004, she also served as Pastor of The Plan Ministries in Greeleyville South Carolina. In 2004, Pastor Angela joined partnership with Faith Tabernacle Ministries, under the leadership of Apostle Bill and Marsha Burns in Kremmling Colorado.

In 2010, she became a council member for Prophetic Intercessors Council of Empowered People (PICEP), under the leadership of Elder Monique Simmons, Kingdom Harvest Ministries in Landover Maryland.

She has two wonderful children Vincent and Tonoah.

CHAPTER 4

Breathe Worship

In the heavens, the Lord created the Angels to worship him. They cry out Holy, Holy, Holy! Is the Lord God Almighty all Day. **(Isaiah 6:2-3).**

Can you Imagine what would happen if God's people decided to create a constant atmosphere of unlimited pure worship all day? Imagine Him sitting upon the throne High lifted up, and His train filling the temple. Beautiful beyond anything you have ever seen errand in splendor right before your very eyes. Just the mere thought should immediately change our posture. What if we lost track of time and we got so caught in the heavenly realms of the Spirit and His people began to cry out to Him. He is Holy All daylong breathing in the sweet smell of His aroma.

We need to remember that we are the human form of His speaking spirits here on the earth **(Genesis 1:27).** We are created in the image and likeness of our Lord. We are seated in heavenly places with Christ Jesus. Our bodies are the temple of the Lord. I remember one Saturday at Intercessory prayer, the prayer warriors decided to do what the angels were doing in heaven according to the word

of God. We started to walk by each other swiftly and crying out HE
is HOLY!

We cried out constantly to each other as we passed by one
another. Every time we would say He is Holy, another realm of the
spirit of God fell. We literally didn't know where we were. We do not
even know how we got to our cars that day. The next day when we
came to the regular Sunday service, the spirit realm was still heavy
in the atmosphere. Every time we would say, He is Holy! Someone
would hit the floor.

It was like you were stepping in rivers of living water. People
were laying everywhere. Some people said they saw visions of angels.
Some were weeping under chairs. There were some of us laying out
just resting in the peace of the Lord. We definitely were slain in the
spirit. We were in awe of what was happening. Anything you wanted
to receive that day would have come to pass, healing, deliverance; all
you had to do was grab it. My God what a time we had in the Lord.
Someone said something to me some months ago that has still stuck
with me today. They said you breathe worship. I thought to myself
what are you saying to me Lord. Then, I was reminded by the sweet
Holy Spirit of what our Lord and Savior has done.

Everywhere we go when we look at His wonderful creation
(John 1:3) we should sing of His goodness, mercy and loving
kindness towards us because they are new every day. What does it
mean to breathe worship? Every second of every day, think about
how Jesus saved our lives and delivered you from something. Just
think about how Jesus came to earth was a living sacrifice for us and
died on the cross. We all have the gift of eternal life with Him

in heaven. Let us Worship him! When you think about how He snatched you from a burning hell, you should worship Him. When we breathe in fresh air, we should breathe out worship, giving Him glory and honor for what He has done.

There are certain actions of posture we can take to put us into a place of Worship. In some countries when you come before a king, you have to kneel down. It shows a posture of Reverence and Adoration for the king. Sometimes you have get into a position of lying prostrate before the Lord. You can also worship with our Lord by singing to him. David would sing and dance before the Lord daily. If you want to draw closer to the Lord, ask the Holy Spirit to give you a heart for worship. Our bodies are an instrument for the Lord. *"Those that worship him must worship him in spirit and in truth"* **(John 4:24 NKJV)**.

One of the first Commandments in the book of Deuteronomy 5:7-8 is to Worship the True and Living God and to serve him only. We should have a daily lifestyle of worship just because of who He is (Elohim, My Creator). Worship our Lord and only Him shall you serve He is a Jealous God **(Deuteronomy 4:23-24)**. Don't put your trust in money, or people, and positions of power in this world because all things will past way one day, but the word of the Lord will always rule and reign forever. When you reference the scriptures below look at how the Lord drew might kings to Himself. He shifted people lives through worship and brought change, healing and deliverance in them.

1.) Worship can will draw people to King Jesus **(Matthew 2:1-2) (Isaiah 66:23).**

2.) When you give the Lord a sacrificial precious gift of worship He will always remember what you did and keep it dear to His heart (**Matthew 26:7-9).**

3.) Worship will cleanse you of issues and set you free **(Matthew 8:2-3).**

4.) Worship will cause your flesh to die and be a living sacrifice to God and to reverence him as Lord over everything. **(Genesis 22:2:8).**

5.) Worship will strengthen you and thrust you into a boldness to go forth to do the works in the Kingdom of God **(Philippians 4:13).**

Everything we do should be a sacrifice of worship to our Lord, the mighty King of Glory! *"¹Give unto the Lord, O you Mighty ones, Give unto the Lord Glory and Strength. ²Give unto the Lord the Glory due his name. Worship the Lord in the Beauty of Holiness!"* **(Psalm 29:1-2 NKJV).**

There was a time in my life as a pregnant teenage girl I was so broken, rejected and lost I decided to take my life. No one in my family knew what I was going to do. I remember getting on my knees one day and saying to God "If you are such a good, kind and loving God why don't I see it in my life. Everything I do seem to fail." If this is the kind of love, you show to your people I do not want to live anymore. I had decided that day I was going to take my life the next week. When that next week came, my mom told me we were going to have a visitor.

I never knew until that day that I had another sister that

was a little older than I was. She was coming to live with us for a while. She was a born again believer of Christ and we began to have a close relationship. She began to minister to me about the Gospel of Jesus Christ. She told me how much He loved me and wanted me to have the gift of eternal life. She started going to a Christian church in Washington DC. I started attending with her one Sunday. Every person I met that day showered me with love. I had never experienced a group of people who knew nothing about me, to embrace me that way. The love of Christ in them drew me closer to Him. I wanted to have that same love so I dedicate my life to Christ Jesus. I was baptized and became a born again believer. The devil thought he was going to kill my unborn child and me but truly, my Lord had another plan for my life. *"For I know the thoughts that I think toward you, saith the Lord, thoughts of peace, and not of evil, to give you an expected end."* **(Jeremiah 29:11 KJV).** I am a living witness of how much our Lord Jesus Christ loves us and wants us to have an abundant life. I could have been in a burning hell, but He saved a wrench like me. This is the reason why I serve Him and worship Him daily. It does not matter how we feel our posture always will be in a place of adoration to the King of Glory just because of who He is. He is Lord over everything!

If you want the Heart of God, become a worshipper. I am reminded of how the Lord said to King David that he was a man after His own heart. Even though, he would do things in his life that displeased the Lord as many of us do every day, he would repent of his sins and continue to do the work of the Lord. **(Psalm 51:9-13).** King David never stopped giving glory and honor to God. The Lord loved him so much because he was a worshipper. He wanted to please the Lord *"¹²And it was King David saying, The Lord hath blessed the house of Obededom, and all that pertaineth unto him, because of the ark of God. So David went and brought up the ark of God from the house of Obededom into the city of David with gladness. ¹³And it was so, that when they bare the ark of the Lord had gone six paces, he sacrificed oxen and fatlings. ¹⁴And David danced before the Lord with all his might and David was girded with a linen ephod. ¹⁵So David and all the house of Israel brought up the ark of the Lord with shouting, and with the sound of the trumpet."* **(II Samuel 6:12-16 KJV)**. Position yourself in worship and the Lord will take you higher in the spirit realm! When you worship the Lord, you are telling God who He is to you.

MY PRAYER

You are sovereign Lord. You are King of Kings and Lord of Lords, Surely You are the King of Glory! Holy in all Your ways Lord, Blessed be the true and living God. Holy and Righteous are You Lord. You are the Risen Savior and Master of every living thing. Blessed be the true and living God. Blessed be the lamb of the living God. Holy, Holy, Holy, Holy are you Lord. You are our Redeemer! You are the Lord of hosts and the Lion of Judah, The God of Abraham, Isaac, and Jacob. We are grateful to you Lord that Your mercies are new every day. Help your people to worship you Lord in spirit and in truth. Help us to honor You in all that we say and do Lord. We repent of our wicked ways Lord and turn to Your ways to let You rule and reign in our hearts.

We desire to be overcomers in our lives by the word of the living

God. You Lord are our present help in the times of trouble. We thank You Lord for being the lifter of our head and helping us to stay on the straight and narrow path of righteousness. Help us to walk in Your word daily and let Your will be done in our lives. Let us live as living sacrifices to You Lord. Let our posture always be a position of humbleness and reverence to You, Oh mighty King. Let the hope of our calling be in Your timing and not ours. Let us come to an understanding Lord that we are a great people with great power!

Serving our God Jehovah all the days of our Lives. Knowing in our hearts that You will never leave us or forsake Your people Lord. We will be a faithful people to Your word, and love our neighbors as we love ourselves like You have commanded us to do. Lord help us to pray for our enemies that they will come into the knowledge and understanding of Your will for their lives and be saved, set free and filled with the Holy Ghost. Let your people do great and mighty works on the earth as it has done already in heaven. Show us Lord, how to have a spirit of boldness and disciple others for Your Kingdom; that we may carry out the great Commission and go forth with a willing heart into the highways and byways of the earth to proclaim the everlasting word of the Lord Jesus Christ. So, that others may come to a full knowledge and understanding of who they are in Christ Jesus.

Lord Jesus help us to not lean to our own understanding; but acknowledge You in all of our ways; so that You may direct our paths. We decree and declare that Your will and Your ways will overpower anything that You would have us to do for You Lord. In the precious name of the Lord Jesus Christ, we seal this prayer with the Blood of Jesus Christ. Amen!

THERESA HIGGS

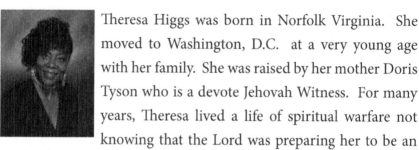

Theresa Higgs was born in Norfolk Virginia. She moved to Washington, D.C. at a very young age with her family. She was raised by her mother Doris Tyson who is a devote Jehovah Witness. For many years, Theresa lived a life of spiritual warfare not knowing that the Lord was preparing her to be an intercessor for the Kingdom of God. At a very critical time in her life, Theresa wanted to commit suicide; but the merciful Lord decided to send her help through her beloved older sister, Deloris Veney (now deceased). It was through the ministering of her sister that she came to know the Lord Jesus Christ and was introduced to Evangel Cathedral, in Upper Marlboro, MD in 1982, where she answered the call of the Lord and was baptized.

By the leading of the Holy Spirit and under, the leadership and legacy of the Honorable Bishop John L. Meares, Theresa furthered her love relationship with the Lord. Today, Theresa is still a member of Evangel Cathedral and serves under, Bishop Donald D. Meares. For 12 years, Theresa also served, under the leadership of Elder/ Prophet Peyton Gray in a thriving youth ministry where he taught his leadership how to go higher in the Lord.

In March 2009, Theresa led a bible class in Evangel's Bible School for teenage girls overseen by Elder Kevin Matthews.

Theresa is the Founder of 'Three-D-Power-N-U', a non-profit ministry that empowers young girls/ladies to reach their highest potential in the Lord and in life. Theresa is anointed in winning souls for the Kingdom of God wherever she goes. She is also a dedicated counselor at the Capitol Hill Pregnancy Center in Washington DC for the past four years. Theresa's posture in life is to be worshipper of the Lord and to do His will on earth. She has four wonderful sons, Damar, Shawn (foster son), Eugene Jr., and Justin.

CHAPTER 5

A Woman of Righteousness
The Book of Esther Chapters 1-2

Righteousness (defined by Wikipedia Website) – righteous, integrity, truth, sincere, just or lawful.

The Bible depicts many Godly women, Esther is one that is describes such a woman. She was also known as Hadassah, which means myrtle, myrtle branches signify peace and thanksgiving (The Living Word Library). She exposes the character of being a righteous woman. There were no miracles done in her presence. But through Esther's faithful character, God's redeeming plan and His powerful, merciful and faithful hand; Esther became God's instrument for His people. God's name was absent from the page of this book, but He is present in every scene within the activities of every event. Not that God had to, but He proved that He is indeed, Lord of His people, the Jews. This is also true with us, it may seem God is distant or not there, He really is, because God said, "...I will never leave thee, nor forsake thee" (Hebrews 13:5b).

Now, let's take a closer look at Esther, she was an orphan taken in by her uncle Mordecai and his wife. Her parents had died, and as a result I can imagine that Esther went through separation, bitterness, and negative emotions; filled with grief, anger, heartbroken and insecurity. Like, any young girl separated from her family and friends, Esther bought all her issues with her when she was brought to King Xerxes palace, as one of the virgin girls in preparation for the future queen. Esther had to go through twelve months of beauty treatments and some readings say twelve months of purification before meeting the king. God's preparation for Esther was more than just soaking in the oil of myrrh for six months, and perfumes the other six months; it was to save His chosen people, the Jews. Our lives are no different today. I believe before we go into the presence of our King (God); we need to do some preparation. As women of righteousness, we should take a look at our conduct and what have we done prior to going into God's presence by asking these questions:

- Were we involved in gossip?
- Were we bitter towards someone?
- Did we cause division with a family member, a Christian brother/sister, or co-worker?
- Did we deal with anger or did we just come off an emotional rollercoaster in our minds, which may have caused us to miss the mark in representing ourselves as women of righteousness? Subsequently, because we chose to leave on the garment of the old man and left the new self hanging out there waiting?

Recognizing, there are times that it is hard for us to follow the direction of the new you; because we are not used to waiting on the direction that is leading us in the right way. We must understand that the Word of God will show us the right way to go, if we yield to its teaching in the knowledge that Jesus is the Way, the truth, and the life. When we follow the right way, the Word will keep us immersed in righteousness and holiness. In Ephesians 4:24 (NIV), it tells us "to put on the new self; created to be like God in true righteousness and holiness." Righteousness describes doing something, what have we done or caused doing the course of the day. Has guilt and conviction pierced our hearts, before we go into God's presence. Ezra 9:15 (NIV) states, "O LORD, God of Israel, you are righteous! We are left this day as a remnant. Here we are before you in our guilt, though because of it not one of us can stand in your presence." Did we represent the gift of righteousness, giving to us from God to man? Esther preparation for the purification took place for six months using oil of myrrh and six other perfumes. Doing the time of the purification, Esther body was rubbed with the perfumes. Can you imagine all those aromas coming together to make its' own fragrance? She was taken to the bathhouse to soak, to remove all the impurities in her body. Today, I would call this detoxification. The oil of myrrh was used to get rid of bitterness, grief and provocation. Provocation is when one is provoked and anger swells up on the inside; their hearts are harden, and it causes one to disobey the voice of the Lord. Life itself, does not deal us a hand that we can handle at time. There are times, we will have to deal with one hurt after another, hurts from a family member, friend children, grandchild, a spouse, or a co-worker, and the hurt, which causes us to become bitter and angry. And through it all, these hurts are permitted and become our trials and tribulations; which test us, in order to bring God glory. We may or will not like when we are dealing with the hurt. However, in spite of, I believe God wants our lips to glorify Him. Psalm 63:3 states, "Because your love is better than life, my lips will glorify you" and Psalm 69:30 states, "I will praise God's name in song and glorify him with thanksgiving."

I believe when we glorify God it will allow us to see Him and not the problem; it will cause us to magnify who He is. And He is bigger than all of our issues and problems, but we have to believe it ourselves. We have to allow our faith, to have faith in God, allow our trust, to trust in God, allow our belief, to believe in the Word of God and take root in our heart. Here are just a few scriptures that bring clarity to what was just stated: "So then faith comes by hearing, and hearing by the Word of God" (Romans 10:17). "Trust in the Lord with all your heart and lean not on your own understanding" (Proverbs 3:5). Yet to all who received him, to those who believed in his name, he gave the right to become children of God (Refer to John 1:12).

I believe before Esther's purification was completed, she knew, who God was through prayer, and she began to hear the voice of God. In Deuteronomy 30:20 it states, "You may love the Lord your God, listen to his voice and hold fast to Him, For the Lord is your life." In Psalm 66:19, "But God has surely listened and heard our voice in prayer and in Hebrews 3:7 states, "Today, if you hear his voice, do not harden your hearts." God was not mention in this book, but I believe he became the God of her life. I believe he heard Esther through her silent prayers and her heart was no longer hardened towards Him. The Lord sees our hearts, because our hearts are deceitful, and He wants us to have a heart to love him, and seek Him with all of our heart. I believe this will happen, when we allow the Lord to mend our heart.

Now, that Esther heart was ready to receive the Word of God, I believe she was willing to say yes Lord, to her assignment. She was transformed from a woman of fear to a woman of faith, one that will walk in righteousness and in holiness, to rule in the palace and above all to save the Jews. When we look at the word righteousness and holiness; you can't have one without the other. Emmet Ministries describe these two words, so much that when you look at one of the words, you look at righteousness, you will als0 see holiness. Holiness is ones' character, righteousness is our conduct. Neither one of them can be separated from the other; they are as intimately related as root and fruit. You cannot get a fruit, if you don't have a root. There can be no righteousness, unless there is holiness. The bible tells us no man can see God without holiness, the Word of God tells us just as he who called you is holy, so be holy in all you do; "for it is written: Be holy, because I am holy"(1 Peter 1:16, NIV). When we are living holy it is not for the present, it is for our future, eternal life and it does not cost us anything to live holy, except to live righteous (NIV Commentary).

Through all of Esther transformation, purification and, sanctification, she became a woman of righteousness, whom was an ordinary woman with the uncommon, extraordinary favor of God in her life. As a single woman, she did not waste any time sitting on the sidelines. But she used her time wisely; especially being the woman God wanted her to be (Charo & Paul Washer). She carried out her duties without regards of how people would look at her. People may not understand why you are so committed and consistent about your duty or duties you have been assigned. And there is no need, trying to explain; some people will not understand the move of God that is on your life. However, one thing I do know is when it is your season; work at it, keep digging into the ground until you see fruit blossom for the glory of God. We have to learn as well, if it is not your season, still do ministry. We have to work in season and out of season. As we look at the natural season and when it is time for the season to change, it changes; which is not to be confused to what needs to be done. However, in the spirit, we need to know what season we are in.

Esther did not let her outer beauty become an obstacle. I believe when Esther looked at herself, she saw how pretty she was, but did not become vain about her looks. On the other hand, some women get carried away with their outer beauty; which one day will fade away. It is the inner self, the unfading beauty of a gentle and quiet spirit, which is of great worth in God's sight. For this, is the way the holy women of the past, who put their hope in God used to make themselves beautiful (Refer to I Peter 3:4-5). And she did not use her beautiful appearance to get her way in the palace. She didn't argue, boast or fight. She realized it was the inner beauty transformation that caused her to be the chosen queen. Esther was not arrogant or full of pride. Sometimes, when we allow God to use us; some can become arrogant and full of pride. When arrogance is displayed, we have put on a show to display to people how conceited we can become. Have we forgotten that every good and perfect gift comes from above? And it is God that will give each one, just as He determines (NIV Commentary). God in His sovereignty determines which gift or gifts each believer should have. Esther, a woman of righteousness, pushed past her fears and looked to the benefits for others. She conquered her fears to become a champion. She was known as a heroine woman. She was not concerned about her own life, as she was for the lives of her people. The Jews were set up for genocide. Haman and the boys wanted to take the Jews out; leaving not one person to talk about it.

There was great mourning among the Jews, with fasting, weeping and wailing as mentioned in the latter portion of Esther 4:3, "…many lay in sackcloth and ashes." There are times; we have to take a stand against the spirit of genocide used by the spirit of darkness. These spirits has been assigned to take some family members out through street gangs, drugs, alcohol, prostitution, homelessness, mental problems, and the list goes on. But through your love, faithfulness and your courage; a stand has to be made, in order for some things to be broken. It must be done through prayer and with fasting. Isaiah 58:-6-8(NIV) states, "Is not this the king of fasting I have chosen: to loose the chains of injustice and untie the cords of the yoke, to set the oppressed free and break every yoke? Is it not to share your food with the hungry and to provide the poor wanderer with shelter when you see the naked, to clothe him, and not to turn away from your own flesh and blood? Then, your light will break forth like the dawn, and your healing will quickly appear; then your righteousness will go before you, and the glory of the Lord will be your rear guard."

Even, when we don't want to be bothered with our family members; we have to show love. It is the outward evidence of genuine righteousness they need to see. No matter what, they are still your flesh and blood, and for such a time as this, you are assigned to stand in the gap for them, and sound the trumpet with your voice like Esther, "…and if I perish, I perish" (Esther 4:16b). It is you, woman of righteousness, called to stand in the gap between Satan and man or between God and man. So, equip yourselves and get into His presence, humble yourself, lift up holy hands unto the Lord, guard your heart, and wait for your print out of your assignment. Esther was a picture of courage and hope to all women that may feel powerless and priceless. As women, we may feel powerless, but we are powerless without Jesus Christ giving us powers; the one who is all powerful. And we may seem priceless, as righteous women of God; no one can put a price on our life. We were already bought with a price, the blood of Jesus the Christ our Lord and Savior.

Remember, righteousness and holiness go together. "You cannot separate one from the other, it is just like the ocean needs the water, like a kite needs the wind or a baby need its mother" (Sheryl Brady). The world tells us we live to learn, but we should learn to live.

PRAYER

Father, thank You for Your favor and for everything you've done for me. I commit my life to you. Use me for Your Kingdom and glory. In Jesus Christ' name. Amen.

ELDER BARBARA SMITH

Elder Barbara Smith is a native of Baltimore, Maryland. She is married to Elder Kenneth Smith; she is a virtuous woman, mother, grandmother and dedicated servant of God. During the time she served as a faithful member of Sacred Zion Full Gospel Baptist Church, under the leadership of Elder Dr. Bertha Green, who is now Bishop. Elder Smith received her call in June of 1997 to the gospel of ministry. This is when she preached her trial sermon. She has since allowed God to order her footsteps in the ministry.

Elder Smith is now serving at Praise the Lord Ministries under the leadership of Pastor Michael Reynolds. As a result of her moving to this place of worship and fellowship, and eight years as a servant; she now oversees the outreach ministry and a servant to the women ministry under Deborah Reynolds. She was ordained as an elder on the 25th of June 2010, by the authority and order of the Province of St. John International Community of Christian Churches in Woodbridge, Virginia.

Elder Barbara Smith is a graduate of Edmondson High School, attended Family Bible Seminary School and G.L.A.D.D. Bible College, where she received a Counseling Certificate on July 25, 1998. She was an intercessor at Sacred Zion Full Gospel Church, and she ministered at the Women Pre-Release Center in Baltimore, Maryland. She has a heart for winning souls and spreading the gospel to the lost, rejected, brokenhearted, and those who are held captive to the world of darkness. She loves to preach and teach the Word of God.

As a faithful servant of Jesus Christ, she knows that it's through God's strength and power that allows her to stand, believe, and trust Him. She gives all praise, glory and honor to God for calling her to birth a Word in the nation.

One of her favorite scriptures is Isaiah 55:11 (Life Application Bible), "So also is my Word. I send it out and it always produces fruit. It shall accomplish all I want it to, and prosper everywhere I send it." She wants to continue to reach the masses by the leadership and guidance of her Heavenly Father, the grace of Jesus Christ and the anointing power of the Holy Spirit.

CHAPTER 6

Holiness

When it comes to holiness, any topic concerning God and His Word is inexhaustible. This is just the tip of the iceberg concerning God's holiness and the holiness of His people. God has given His commandment, ***"Be ye holy; for I am holy."*** **(I Peter 1:16 KJV).** Yet if one were to look at the present condition of the body of Christ, it would be doubtful to believe that God has given His people this command. The church has allowed the world to influence it to such a degree that we can't distinguish between the two. We live in an unholy world and are confronted with unholiness daily. However, God has promised, ***"When the enemy comes in like a flood; the Spirit of the Lord will lift up a standard against him."*** **(Isaiah 59:19 KJV).** God's people are the standard. It may be difficult to live holy in an unholy world. God would not have given us a command if He had not made provisions and a way to live by them.

Holiness is not a denomination, it is not a long black dress, no make-up, hair pulled back in a bun or no jewelry. It is not speaking in tongues with your hands lifted up. These things do not constitute holiness. God is holy; He is separate from all other beings. He is pure, clean, spotless, and untainted with evil. God's holiness is absolute; it has no limits and no degrees.

I believe of all Gods attributes and characteristics the holiness of God is preeminent. *"The Lord is righteous in all His ways and holy to all His works."* **(Psalm 145:17 KJV)**.

The scripture states, *"Who is like unto thee, O Lord among the gods? Who is like thee, glorious in holiness, fearful in praises, doing wonders?"* **(Exodus 15:11 KJV)**. Solomon in his wisdom answered, "There is none like thee", and Moses in his meekness answered the same. What God is like our God? What God is there that can part a sea and allow His people to walk through on dry land? What God could speak the universe into existence? What God could provide Himself as a perfect sacrifice and the world continue its' course? There is no god like our God.

Paul's writing to the Corinthians said there is one God, and though there are many that are called gods or idols unto Christians there is one God. We, as sons of God have this knowledge; but not all have this knowledge, the knowledge of God. Our God separates Himself from all other gods. Let us look at some of the qualities of our God.

First, our God is Jehovah. He is the self-existent one, the eternal one. He did not originate in someone's mind, nor was he carved out of stone. Genesis 1:1 states, *"In the beginning God created the heaven and the earth."* **(Genesis 1:1 KJV)**. David declared in **Psalm 91**, *"¹He that dwelleth in the secret place of the most high (Elelyon) shall abide under the shadow of the Almighty (El Shaddai), ²I will say of the Lord (Jehovah), He is my refuge and my fortress, my God (Elohim), in Him will I trust in the Lord, Jehovah, the self-existent one.* **(Psalm 91:1-2 KJV)**. Secondly, our God forgives sins. When the man who had palsy was lifted down through the roof, Jesus stated that his sins were forgiven **(Mark 2:2-5)**. Thirdly, our God dwells not just in the midst of His people, but He dwells within us. Jesus said if any hear His voice and open the door, He would come in to him and have fellowship with him. These are just a few qualities that separate our God from other gods, can you think of any?

TO WHOM IS THE HOLINESS OF GOD REVEALED?

The holiness of God is revealed in the contrite and humble in spirit. *"For thus saith the high and lofty One that inhabiteth eternity, whose name is Holy; I dwell in the high and holy place with him also that is of a contrite and humble spirit, to revive the spirit of the humble , and to revive the heart of the contrite ones."* **(Isaiah 57:15 KJV)**. God's holiness is revealed to the meek. The Bible says that Moses was very meek above all men, which were upon the face of the earth **(Numbers 12:3)**. Like Moses, we have to move out of the way to see the holiness of God.

God's holiness is revealed to demons and unclean spirits. So, how much more of His holiness is revealed to those who have been washed in the blood of Jesus and who are pursuing holiness? The more we seek the face of God, the more of His holiness we will see.

WHAT HAPPENS WHEN WE RECOGNIZE THE HOLINESS OF GOD?

Isaiah said in the year that King Uzziah died, he saw God high and lifted up and His train filled the temple. He saw the angels worshipping God and crying, Holy, Holy is the Lord of hosts. After seeing this Isaiah said, *"Woe is me! For I am undone! Because*

I am a man of unclean lips." **(Isaiah 6:5 KJV)**. Like Isaiah, when we recognize the holiness of God we will recognize the sin in our lives as well as in others around us.

God's holiness will not only make us see our sin and shortcomings, but also will cause us to repent. Job said, *"5I have heard of thee by the hearing of the ear, but now my eyes seeth thee! 6Wherefore I abhor myself and repent in dust and ashes."* **(Job** 42:5-**6 KJV)**. God's holiness will cause us to hate evil and sin as He does. *"Ye that love the Lord hate evil; He preserveth the souls of his saints; He delivereth out of hand of the wicked. Light is sown for the righteous, and gladness for the upright in heart. Rejoice in the Lord ye righteous; and give thanks at the remembrance of His holiness."* **(Psalm 97:10 KJV)**.

When we recognize the holiness of God, we will be moved to purify ourselves. *"2Beloved. Now are we the sons of God and it doth not yet appear what we shall be: but we know that, when he shall appear, we shall be like Him; for we shall see Him as He is. 3And every man that hath this hope in him purifieth himself, even as He is pure."* **(I John 3:2-3 KJV)**. This cycle of purifying should be present in our lives daily.

THE PURSUIT OF HOLINESS

God demands holiness for the New Testament believers just as He did for the children of Israel. *"I am the Lord your God which have separated you from other people"* **(Leviticus 20:24 KJV)**. Verse 26 of the same chapter reads *"And ye shall be holy unto me: For I the Lord am holy and have severed you from* *other people, that you should be mine"* **(Leviticus 20:26 KJV)**. The New Testament puts it this way, *"You have been bought with a price, therefore glorify God in your body and in your spirit which belong to God."* **(I Corinthians 6:20 KJV)**.

PRESENTING YOUR BODIES

Romans 12:1-2 is familiar to all of us. Paul writing to the Church at Rome states, *"¹I beseech ye therefore, brethren by the mercies of God, that ye present your bodies a living sacrifice, holy, acceptable unto God, which is your reasonable service. ²And be ye not conformed to this world; but be ye transformed by the renewing of your mind, that ye may prove what is that good, and acceptable, (well pleasing) and perfect, will of God."* **(Romans 12:1-2 KJV)**.

The sacrifice we offer to God, which is our body, must be acceptable to Him. We cannot offer it in any way we think might be suitable. In Paul's day, the sacrifices that were presented to God were supposed to be pure and spotless. To be holy means to be set apart for God. When we have been set apart by God, it means that we have left our sin behind. Sin no longer controls our lives. We no longer love sin. Yet, when we do happen to sin, we should repent and determine in our hearts to follow Christ. Holiness should be important to Christians. We should strive to be holy and look for holiness in others while encouraging one another to live holy lives. God wants us to offer a holy sacrifice. If we do as Paul says to do "present your bodies as a living sacrifice, holy unto God" our sacrifice will be holy and acceptable by God.

Malachi 1:6-10 lets us know how God felt when there was

a blemish in the sacrifice that the priests were offering at the altar. When Aarons' sons offered up strange fire unto God, they were consumed. Moses then said to Aaron, "the Lord spoke saying, by those who come near me, I will be treated holy. We cannot offer our bodies to God in any way we choose. God is holy and our bodies are the temple of God and should be treated as such.

IN CONCLUSION

God wants us to be holy because it becomes us. *"Thy testimonies are very sure: holiness becomes thine house, O Lord, forever."* **(Psalm 93:5 KJV)**. *"We are being build up into a spiritual house, an holy priesthood to offer up spiritual sacrifices acceptable to God by Jesus Christ."* **(I Peter 2:5 KJV)**. When the Father sees us living holy, He recognizes how good we look. What father would not want to see like qualities in his son? It is therefore only right that we should be holy because we have been created in His image, which is righteousness and holiness.

God wants us to be holy so we can manifest His presence in this world. God's presence is everywhere, but His presence is not manifested everywhere. **Romans 8:19, 22**, declares that the whole creation groans and eagerly waits for the manifestation of the sons of God. God wants a vessel unto honor, meet, suitable for His use. God wants to be exalted among the heathen and it will take His people, whom He has separated and who are pursuing holiness to do this.

While it may be difficult at times to be holy in an unholy world, let us not forget whose we are and that God is for us and not against us. *"[1]Wherefore seeing we also are compassed about with so great a cloud of witnesses, let us lay aside every weight , and sin which doth so easily beset us, and let us run with patience the race that is set before us, ²looking unto Jesus the author and finisher of our faith…"* **(Hebrews 12:1-2 KJV)**.

We have a cloud of witnesses that have gone before us, lived a holy life and received their rewards. With this in mind, let us not faint nor lose heart. Let us continue to look unto Jesus, who is the author and perfecter of our faith. The one who is our helper, builder, and rewarder; He is our all in all. Let us diligently pursue holiness, without which one will not see God.

"For I know the thoughts that I think toward you saith the Lord, thoughts of peace, and not evil, to give you an expected end." **(Jeremiah 29:11 KJV).** Remember, Saints Holiness Becometh Your House!

ELDER BERTHA STEWARD

Greetings, in the holiness of our true and living God! I am a member of the Woodlawn Christian Fellowship in Woodlawn, Maryland.

I am under the leadership of Pastors Thomas and Michele Perrera. I can tell you all you need to know about me in one word, "bondservant" of the most High God. I am a 'bondservant' who wants to stay connected to my Master and who serves out of love and liberty.

CHAPTER 7

Who are you? Where did you come from?

I want to first thank God today for the ability to minister to every man, woman, boy and girl. It was the thorns of my life that caused conception to take place. I also want to thank Virginia Johnson for this piece of writing and I thank her because if it were not for our conversations one evening, today would not be possible. Thanks Virginia!

Prayer is to address God in adoration, confession, supplication, or thanksgiving: to intercede. Deception is to lead astray, to cause to accept as true what is false, fraud, trickery, lying, not honest, misleading, deceptive, something that deceives, trick; the act of deceiving.

My friend was talking to me about her house that she liked very much. During the process of purchasing this house, someone recommended that she get the house inspected, before even signing or going into this house. As I, was standing there listening to her talk about what the housing inspector found, something on the inside of me said, um? That is prayer or at least one of the things that Prayer is for, and that is to do a thorough inspection of a thing, person, place, etc. As I stood there listening to her, a revelation began to open up like never before about prayer! Prayer is a sifter; it separates what is true and what is not true. I began to reflect over my life and God showed me that in several choices I made I never consulted him and in the end, the choice proved painful.

The housing inspector is trained to see what we do not see. When we are so caught up in how the outside of something appears, we are not clearly thinking about the hidden things that could potentially cause great harm "down the road." The housing inspector is specifically trained to watch out and look for problem areas. They are trained to look underneath and behind areas that potential homeowners overlook. After going through the house from top to bottom with a fine toothcomb, the housing inspector then advises you of the potential problems and whether or not the house is a suitable investment. They advise you if the house will bring you joy or sorrow.

Prayer is the same way. Prayer is our personal inspector. It does for us what we cannot do or really what we cannot see. I keep driving the point that the "unseen" is more dangerous than what we give credit. As new homeowners, we are looking at the curtains, decorations, and the colors that will go good together. However, when the inspector goes in, pulls back a layer of dry wall, and reveals mold; then you are like wait a minute.

This brings us to our "homily"for today. A homily is a word of Encouragement from the Lord. In **Joshua 9:1-27** scripture, we have Joshua as the leader with the Israelites just came out of winning a battle. You know how it is when you have won something, and it is advertised all over; other people heard of the great victory of Joshua. Be careful after great victories because the enemy is sure to show up. The enemy will use anyone who is willing to be used against you.

The Israelites were approached by foreign people that out of nowhere asked for a treaty or asking to be helped. These people pretended to be something that they were not so, that they would receive help from Joshua and the children of Israel. Let us focus on this for just one second because this is an example from Joshua where we all have gotten tricked one way or the other, because we do not inquire of the Lord. The Israelites asked a question, "How do we know you and do you live nearby?" In order, for one to ask such questions, means that you have some reservations, or uncertainties. For example, suppose a loved one passes and you come into a large amount of wealth and all of a sudden, folk you have not seen in years or so called other sibling shows up. What do you do? Would you blindly trust people you do not even know? I often go back to a sermon of Pastor Susie Owens, whom I love because she is very upfront in her preaching. She says I am going to know why you want to be in my life. What is your true motive or intention of wanting to be in my life? Prayer does this very thing. It gives God permission to sift the hearts of people. In Verse 14 the text says, *"The Israelites examined the food, but they did not consult the Lord."* **(Joshua 9:14 NLT)**. If I can minister and pour out of my heart today, if you hear nothing else, please listen to me. It was not the food that should have been of great importance but the motive of the heart, the intentions of why they were there.

Prayer is your weapon of warfare. Prayer intercedes and goes out to sift and shake up what is not right. Prayer should be considered before doing anything life changing, such as marriage, signing contracts, buying homes, cars, or anything that is life changing. We should pray the following:

God, because You are the beginning and the ending of a thing, because You are Lord over my life not just when I need money or material things but You are Lord when I can't see the intentions of a person whether Saved or unsaved. I invite You to get involved and search the hearts of those people that are trying to become a part of where You reside in me. While You are sifting, I am waiting for You to authorize this.

You are saying "Lord I give You total permission to inspect the things I cannot see with the naked eye." Let us connect prayer to the familiar, such as a housing inspector is which he or she is trained to check for the hidden things that you are not trained to see. That is prayer and it has the ability to sift and check for the hidden things. Another example we can use is a microscope. Microscopes help us to see things that the naked eye cannot see. Prayer is our microscope!

Joshua decided to take the word of the Gibeonites, then the men of Israel took some of their provisions; but they did not ask counsel of the Lord. Joshua made peace with them, and made a covenant with them to let them live; and the rulers of the congregation swore to them. Now Because, of Joshua's choice, deception was present. When you don't pray, you give the enemy legal right to deceive you. Deception will have you thinking this joker is Godly when he really is not. Deception will have you marrying someone that was not appointed, anointed, ordained, or authorized by God. Marriage is the right thing to do, but if with the wrong person; it is still devastating. Bishop Rudolph Mckissick, Jr. says it better, "you can do the right thing on the wrong mountain."[24] which in other words, you can do the right thing but not with the right person. Marriage is great and honored but to marry and be miserable because you do did not choose the person God has for you. Whether it is a house, job or anything that is God has not authorized it is not His perfect will for you.

I remember living with one of my good friends for about three years named Patrice. In all of the years of living with her, I never saw Patrice make a move without praying. If God did not ok it, she did not care who thought what Patrice never made a move. God proved Himself in her life. Many times, you watch others make decisions that cause them so much hurt and pain. However, when I saw Patrice waiting on the Lord, I knew she was one of the people that I could trust with my life. I knew by her actions that she invited God in her circumstances and that she only moved when He told her to move. Today, Patrice Scott, serves as an example; that prayer is the best tool to seek out His perfect will for your life. At one time in my life I would just do stuff just to do it. I would allow my gift of mercy to be prostituted by people who were greedy. I threw what was precious to God to pigs and swine to the point that at times I did not know if I were coming or going. I was in a state of depression. I put myself in danger countless times because I did not inquire of the Lord about people. I did not consult God about someone that He wanted in my life, so that meant I gave authorization to an unauthorized person; who caused me to become mentally ill. The word of God is a powerful weapon. I don't or try not to make judgments about anyone else. I am a true advocate of allowing people to do whatever they want to do. However (listen to me carefully), you may choose, but after the choice is done and the deed is carried out; God chooses the consequences for you. Man does not choose the consequence! You do not choose the consequence or even how long you will endure it. Even when you pray and God answers no, you must learn to be ok with it. Trust the intentions of God. **Jeremiah 29:11** says the Lord thoughts towards you are of peace and not evil to give you hope. He wants to give all of us an expected end! When you pray, God listens and He feels that you want Him in your life.

As we see in the ending of Joshua, 9:15 "So Joshua made peace with them, and made a covenant with them to let them live; and the rulers of the congregation swore to them". It was not until three days later the bible says in Joshua 9: 16-20 after learning these people were not who they said they were that Joshua promised them safety. Then, Joshua decided to go and investigate who they really were after the treaty was made. Investigation is the beginning and not the ending. Many times, you wait until the promise has been made, the house contract signed and the wedding underway before you decide to investigate and pray. Praying and investigating anything that is life changing does not begin after but in the beginning. This is just a word to the wise.

Prayer in essence gives God a chance to get involved and it shows Him that He is not just savior but Lord over your whole life and we prove this by inviting him in the "unseen" parts that are life-changing events.

"Don't worry about anything; instead, pray about everything." **(Philippians 4:6 NLT)**. Tell God what you need, and thank Him for all He has done.

PRAYER

Lord, there are many things in the world that try to lead man, but I pray that I would be led by Your hand, and that You alone will guide me down the proper path. I know you speak to me in many different ways, so I also ask that when you speak that I will recognize that it is You. Whether it is through a pastor, a friend, a stranger, or directly from Your Word, help me to hear and recognize Your voice, and do Your will. Her Commitment to God can be seen in Joshua 1:14:15 "*"You are to help your brothers until the LORD Gives them rest, as he has done for you, and until they have Taken possession of the land that the LORD your God is giving them. After that, you may go back and occupy your own land, which Moses The servant of the LORD gave you east of the Jordan toward the Sunrise."*

KATINA ENGRAM

Katina Engram is the daughter of the late Reverend Dr. David Lee Jr. and the late Edith Engram. She was born on August 19, 1974 at the former Freedman's Hospital in Washington, D.C. Katina is a native Washingtonian. She attended several schools in the District of Columbia and graduated from Eastern Senior High School in 1992. Katina  made a declaration to submit her life under the authority of our Lord and Savior Jesus Christ, in her early childhood years when she was a member of The Way of the Cross Church in Christ, under the leadership Pastor Alphonso D. Brooks.

In October 2008, Katina received her calling to be an intercessor and minister of the Gospel. Under the leadership of Pastors Jerome and Katina Holmes at Bethel Christian Church in Bowie Maryland, she was installed as a minister-in-training in January 2009.

In 2012, Katina walked in her promise land when she joined the Ministry of The City of Refuge under the leadership of her spiritual father in the Lord, Pastor Glen E. Jenkins and his lovely wife Lady Marguerite Jenkins.

Katina is a Minister in Training where the floodgates have been opened for her to do the will of God in her life and others.

Katina is currently employed at Shirley Contracting, a heavy highway construction company she started in March 2005. Katina formerly worked in the Prince Georges county school system from 2001 -2003 in many capacities including substitute teacher.

Although both of her parents transitioned into glory, Katina continues to honor and cherish their memories. She was especially close to her mother Edith for whom Katina was a lifeline. Katina is grateful for her two brothers, Marcus Lea and Robert Lewis, as well as her stepmother, Patricia Lea.

The Journey Through Prayer Continues

Well, dear readers we are back again with the second installment to our new series entitled "Seven Ingredients to an Effective Prayer Life." Through the reading of this book, you have discovered the next 3 ingredients, which bring us to a total of five ingredients that must effective in your life. The first ingredient is "humility." You must be confident (In GOD), faithful and attentive. We have found out that humility is favorable in God's eyes and is a must to be successful in this Christian walk. This leads me to the second ingredient, which is to "seek." Did you notice the order? One must be humble. You must be first postured correctly in order to seek God and be effective. I know you discovered how to properly seek the Father after you entered into the correct posture of humility. Now, it brings me to the next three ingredients, which are outlined in this book. The third ingredient is True Repentance. You will discover in this book what true repentance really means and how it is to be applied daily in our lives. The forth ingredient is Righteousness, we must always be in right standing with God; the authors will share their experiences on how to obtain and maintain a life of righteousness. Now, the fifth ingredient is Holiness, this is where we get nervous it is not about your outward appearance but your inward parts, which is what truly matters to God. Embrace yourself living a life of holiness. This can be obtained, as you will learn through the reading of this book. I pray that as we continue this journey together that our faith will be renewed and our pray life will increase with passion and fire.

There are two more ingredients to learn about, in order to become completely effective in our prayer life. This is an awesome journey we have embarked upon. I will see you on our next stop of this journey.

I love you more than you will ever know!
Trena

THE VISIONARY

Apostle Designate Trena Stephenson is a gifted preacher, teacher, worship leader, author, playwright, entrepreneur and intercessor. Apostle Designate Trena developed and formed Daughters of Distinction LLC, in 2008, based off her passion for writing and helping others fulfill their passions, as well. Daughters of Distinction  were designed to impact this world with the gospel of Jesus Christ through books, TV and radio ventures. She is a visionary, a woman of great faith, compassion, and integrity. She has been the guest speaker on "The Wenda Royster Show," a radio broadcast of Radio One; Rejoice TV Network; TBN, and Preach the Word Network. In April 2008, Apostle Designate Stephenson became the executive producer and creative director for Daughters of Distinction TV, which houses two shows Daughters of Distinction Live and Let's Talk a new show which, launched in April 2011. Both shows air on Rejoice TV Network in MD and DC. In May 7, 2011, Apostle Designate Stephenson launched The Fullness of God Radio Broadcast airing AL, PA, FL, LA, SC, NC and GA. In September 2010, Apostle Designate Trena also launched Soar Magazine, an online magazine to empower and encourage the people of God. When God opens the door for Apostle Designate Stephenson, she walks through it under the Anointing of the Holy Spirit with the purpose of leading someone to Christ. To learn more about this awesome woman of God you can log onto www.dofdllc.com and www.soarmagazine.info.

RELEASES FROM DAUGHTERS OF DISTINCTION

7 Ingredients to an Effective Prayer Life

Volume 1-2   Volume 3-5

Volume 6-7   Due to Release June 15, 2013

To learn more about the services and upcoming releases go to
www.dofdllc.com
Find us on the web @ www. soarmagazine.info &
www.wofgod.org

REFERENCES

1. "Understanding." n.d. Merriam Webster. Web. 1 Sept. 2012. <http://www.merriam-webster.com/dictionary/understanding>.

2. "Metanoeo." BibleStudyTools.com. Web. 6 Aug. 2012. <http://www.biblestudytools.com/lexicons/greek/kjv/metanoeo.html>

3. "Revelation 3:18." BibleStudyTools.com. Http://www.biblestudytools.com/commentaries/revelation/revelation-3/revelation-3-18.html, n.d. Web. 06 Aug. 2012. <http://www.biblestudytools.com/commentaries/>.

4. "Repent." n.d. Merriam Webster. Web. 1 Sept. 2012. <http://www.merriam-webster.com/dictionary/repent>.

5. The 3 Steps of Repentance." Bible Study Planet. Web. 09 Sept. 2012. <http://biblestudyplanet.com/the-3-steps-of-repentance/>.

6. "Prayer of Repentance." Wikipedia. Wikimedia Foundation, 14 Aug. 2012. Web. 09 Sept. 2012. <http://en.wikipedia.org/wiki/Prayer_of_Repentance>.

7. "sin." Intermediate Dictionary. 5th edition. Glenview, Illinois: Scott, Foresman and Company, 1988. Print

8. Jewish Encyclopedia, 1906, 12 pp. 29 August 2012 http://www.jewishencyclopedia.com/articles/12680-repentance

9. "Image." Merriam Webster Collegiate Dictionary. 10th ed. 1993. Print

10. Briscoe, D. Stuart. *The Fruit of the Spirit: Cultivating Christian character.* Wheaton, IL: H. Shaw, 1993. Print.

11. Kenyon, E. W. Identification: A Romance in Redemption. Lynnwood, WA: Kenyon's Gospel Pub. Society, 1968. Print.

12. Vine, W. E. "Repent." Vines Complete Expository Dictionary. Bath: Thomas Nelson, 1996. Print.

13. "Establish." Webster Seventh New Collegiate Dictionary. Springfield: G.&C. Merriam, 1967. Print.

14. Kenyon, E. W. *Identification: A Romance in Redemption.* Lynnwood, WA: Kenyon's Gospel Pub. Society, 1968. Print.

15. Hammond, Fred. "Call Me Righteous." The Spirit of David. Benson, 1996. CD.

16. Frangipane, Francis. "Holiness Precedes Power." *Ministries of Francis Frangipane.* Web. 19 Sept. 2012. <http://www.frangipane.org/>.

17. Burkett, Bill. "The Most Beautiful Word." *The Most Beautiful Word.* 1996. Web. 7 Aug. 2012. <http://www.actsion.com/beauword.htm>.

18. McKissick, Bishop Rudolph, Jr. *I Am the One.* Bishop Rudolph McKissick Jr. Rec. 07 Mar. 2010. Bishop Rudolph McKissick Jr., 2010. CD.

CPSIA information can be obtained at www.ICGtesting.com
Printed in the USA
BVOW102358070313

315016BV00003B/21/P

9 780983 073550